Delicious recipes everyone will love!

The All Natural

ALLERGY

Cookbook

Dairy-Free

Gluten-Free

Jeanne Marie Martin

THE
All Natural
ALLERGY COOKBOOK

Other books by Jeanne Marie Martin:

Hearty Vegetarian Soups & Stews (Harbour Publishing)
Eating Alive, co-authored with Dr. Jon Matsen
For the Love of Food: The Complete Natural Food Cookbook

THE
All Natural
ALLERGY COOKBOOK

Jeanne Marie Martin

HARBOUR PUBLISHING

Published by
HARBOUR PUBLISHING
P.O. Box 219
Madeira Park, BC Canada V0N 2H0

Cover design by Fiona MacGregor
Drawings by Kelly Brooks
Printed and bound in Canada by Friesen Printers

Canadian Cataloguing in Publication Data

Martin, Jeanne Marie
    The all natural allergy cookbook

    Previously published under title: All natural allergy recipes.
    Includes index.
    ISBN 1-55017-044-9

    1. Gluten-free diet — Recipes. 2. Milk-free diet — Recipes. 3. Food
allergy — Diet Therapy — Recipes. I. Title. II. Title: All natural allergy
recipes.
RC588.D53M37 1991   641.5′631   C91-091328-5

To my dear friend
Karen Waurzyniak-Hogg
who inspired me to experiment with allergy recipes
and provided several of these fine recipes,
including the terrific ice creams

also

special thanks to her husband, Dr. James D. Hogg, D.C.
and their son, Alexander Hogg
for their help.

This book is also dedicated to those who are hungering
for grain recipes they can eat!

Thanks to
Lise Doiron
Viola Pilar, R.N.
Ann Taylor
Goldie Caughlan
for their assistance, support and inspiration,
and to my mother, Lillian M. Martin

CONTENTS

ABOUT
THE
AUTHOR

JEANNE MARIE MARTIN has been sharing her enthusiasm for natural foods for over twenty years, working with thousands of students to prepare delicious, attractive, easy recipes for people with special dietary needs, including arthritis, heart disease, cancer, Candida, veganism, vegetarianism, food sensitivities and allergies.

She taught for six years at a U.S. college, and she has lectured at universities, hospitals and clinics in Canada and the U.S. Jeanne Marie has appeared on numerous television programs, including *Northwest Today, Wake-up* and *Good Company.* Her articles and recipes have been published in *Alive, Natural Living, Healthy Eating* and *Health & Nutrition Update.* She is a regular columnist for *Shared Vision,* a new age magazine, and *Fittingly Yours,* a sports and fitness magazine.

Jeanne Marie's wide experience also includes many years of diet counselling, food demonstrations, food styling and business consulting. She has owned her own catering business in the U.S. and owned and operated a health food store in Thunder Bay, Ontario, and she designed and managed a successful health food store in Vancouver, B.C.

A well-known specialist in nutrition and allergy diets, she currently lives in Vancouver, where she writes, lectures and teaches a wide variety of cooking classes. She works regularly with doctors, naturopaths and other health specialists, advising patients on special diets and menu planning.

For more information on lectures and seminars in North America, write to Jeanne Marie c/o Seminars, Box 4391, Vancouver, B.C. Canada, V6B 3Z8.

WHAT YOU NEED TO KNOW ABOUT THIS BOOK

RECIPES FOR PEOPLE WITH ALLERGIES are plentiful, but they are not always palatable. Dozens of books are available, full of recipes for foods that are acceptable, but far from flavourful. This need not be the case.

I believe there are no bad-tasting foods, only bad recipes. If proper ingredients are blended together in the right proportions, there is no reason why each and every recipe should not be a taste sensation as well as a healthful change from ordinary fare.

A wholesome variety of foods is the basis of a healthful diet. Sometimes a limited, uncreative diet can contribute to a food allergy, because healthful foods are ignored until the body is in trouble. People with food allergies have the opportunity to explore and enjoy a wide assortment of new foods. When health problems arise, it is the time to experiment with more natural recipes, using vegetables, whole grains, legumes, tofu, nuts and seeds.

The most common foods people are allergic to are wheat, corn, gluten (found in wheat, barley, oats and rye), soy, citrus fruits, milk or other dairy products, chocolate, caffeine, sugar, meats, yeast and food additives like flavourings, colourings and preservatives. Recipes for foods without these ingredients are hard to find, especially good breads, cakes, and dairy-free desserts.

If gluten is a problem in your diet, delicious breads and cakes can be made with millet, rice, corn, buckwheat, teff, amaranth, quinoa, tapioca, carob, nut, soy, chick pea, potato, cassava and arrowroot flours. Some people can tolerate gluten in a more digestible form such as kamut or spelt. Millet and rice flour tend to add a slightly bitter taste to foods unless one adds nut milk, fruit juice or spices such as cinnamon, allspice or cardamom. Tapioca, carob or nut flours will also help offset this bitterness.

For those allergic to all grains, amaranth, teff, tapioca, carob, nut, soy, chick pea, cassava, potato and arrowroot flours may be used successfully to make anything, even pancakes, breads and brownies.

Getting gluten-free bread or cake to hold together and rise properly is often a problem, even for the most gifted cook. Eggs or egg substitutes, guar gum, xanthan gum and liquid lecithin can help alleviate these problems.

Those with dairy allergies will find nut, seed, coconut and soy milk wonderful substitutes in recipes for baked goods. They work well in beverages, too. Add a bit of vanilla flavouring and oil, or carob syrup. Fruit juices can also be used quite successfully in place of milk in many recipes.

Tofu works well as a substitute for meat, cheese or cream, and tends to absorb the flavours of whatever it is mixed with. Nutritional yeast may also be used to help create a cheesy flavour in some recipes.

If you are part of the growing number of North Americans with food allergies or temporary food intolerances, search no further. Here are the recipes you have been hungering for, along with kitchen and baking tips, food glossary, storage charts and a product buying guide. *The All Natural Allergy Cookbook* contains recipes for beverages, snacks, soups, main dishes, salads and dressings, cereals, breads and desserts, including substitutes for gluten, grains, eggs, milk and sugar. There is also a suggested book list.

If you have allergies, you have probably had the experience of finding a great recipe that you would love to try, but then finding it is dairy-free but not gluten-free, or vice versa. You will be glad to know that almost every recipe in this book is completely dairy-free *and* gluten-free, and all of them are 100% sugar-free and meat-free.

There are many opinions among health professionals and people with allergies about the causes and treatments of allergies. This book is *not* intended as a medical guide, but as a guide to preparing, serving and cooking delicious, nutritious, easy-to-make foods for people with allergies and food sensitivities.

Most important, you don't have to have an allergy to enjoy cooking and eating the foods in this book. In fact, when you start preparing and serving the wholesome dishes in these pages, you may find your non-allergenic friends asking for seconds and wanting the recipes!

Best wishes and good health!

JEANNE MARIE MARTIN

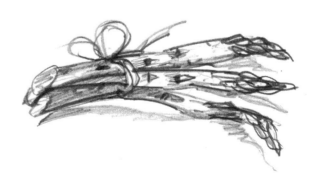

GETTING STARTED

Before You Use These Recipes . . .

Each ingredient in these recipes is specially selected and tested to add texture, consistency or flavour. Avoid changing or rearranging the ingredients, except where variations are suggested, or the recipe may be spoiled. Adding whole wheat flour, for example, may off-balance a bread or cake and cause it to become too sweet or too heavy, or to have an overpowering flavour. On the other hand, it's good to experiment occasionally and learn from experience. Try the recipes without changes or unrecommended substitutions the first time, then experiment gradually.

Because the quality of ingredients can vary, the flavour of each dish may vary slightly as well. Always use the best, freshest ingredients. Choose honey that is flavourful rather than bland, and use 100% *real* maple syrup. Light-coloured, light-tasting cold-pressed oils processed without chemicals are best. Make sure flours are finely ground for the best results in rising.

Measure ingredients carefully and exactly when working with these recipes. Sift dry ingredients together in a separate bowl when directed, and mix ingredients thoroughly.

In short, remember these three rules:

1. Follow recipes carefully.
2. Use high quality ingredients.
3. Measure exactly.

Remember, it is important to enjoy preparing these recipes. Every individual should be able to prepare nourishing foods and discover how exciting cooking can be. Cooking and baking are wonderful adventures, and special *shared* experiences. Once you've tried some of these recipes and had a few successes, you'll love cooking, serving and eating the foods you've prepared with love!

ABOUT THE RECIPES

These recipes contain only natural ingredients and sweeteners. All recipes are wheat-free and dairy-free, and all but a few are free of yeast and gluten as well. Many are prepared without soy or eggs. Some are grain-free, but have a grain-like texture. Substitutes and variations are marked with an asterisk (*). Read each recipe thoroughly before you start cooking, to plan which variation is best for you.

Honey is used frequently in these recipes, but there are alternatives at the end of each recipe. See also Alternative Sweeteners (page 27).

The Food Glossary and Buying Guide at the end of the book will give you important information about food origins and families, qualities and uses, and some tips on where to find the best ingredients.

FOOD AND COOKING TIPS

1. ¾ tsp. sea salt equals 1 tsp. regular table salt. (Regular table salt contains sugar!)
2. For low-salt diets, sea salt amounts may be decreased in recipes *except* bread and cake recipes. Reduce amounts, taste, and add more salt as desired.
3. When doubling a recipe only use 1½ times the amount of salt. When tripling a recipe—double the salt.
4. When oil is used in recipes, try a light-coloured, natural,

cold-pressed variety. As with all natural oil products (including mayonnaise and salad dressings), refrigerate after opening. This is a must for safety and freshness!

5. Kelp (sea kelp) is an important food supplement. It contains iodine and other minerals and sea salt contains no iodine so kelp and sea salt are almost always used together. Kelp also adds flavour and gives body and depth to recipes. Enjoy it often for its many benefits.

6. All nuts and seeds should be chewed very well for proper digestion. Chew them to powder to mix lots of saliva with them and speed digestion.

7. All types of carbohydrate juices like vegetable and non-acidic fruit juices should be sipped very slowly and even swished in the mouth before swallowing to aid digestion and make all the nutrients they contain more easily and completely assimilated. Never gulp juices, savour them. Avoid keeping citrus juices in the mouth, as they may begin to strip the enamel from the teeth.

8. To prevent early spoilage of liquid foods (oil, mayonnaise, dressings, etc.), avoid contaminating them by adding saliva or perspiration, or overexposing them to air. Avoid eating any part of fruits, vegetables, breads or other foods on which mold has begun to grow. Discard any food that may not be fresh.

9. Never undercook or overcook foods. This may impair flavours and digestion. Don't eat foods reheated more than once as they have lost more of their nutrients but retained their calories!

10. Microwaving food does not necessarily kill all bacteria, especially in leftover foods and meats. Stove-top and oven cooking are more likely to kill minor bacteria that may aggravate food sensitivities.

Abbreviations

tsp. teaspoon
Tbs. tablespoon
lb.   pound
oz.   ounce
gm.   gram

Measurements

3 tsp. = 1 Tbs.
4 Tbs. = ¼ cup
8 Tbs. = ½ cup
16 Tbs. = 1 cup
1 oz.   = 2 Tbs.
4 oz.   = ½ cup
8 oz.   = 1 cup

Recipe Symbols

*	variation
E	egg-free
G	gluten-free
S	soy-free
Y	yeast-free
B	baking powder and baking soda–free
Gr	grain-free

Metric Equivalents (approximate)

¼ tsp.	1 mL
½ tsp.	2 mL
1 tsp.	5 mL
1 Tbs.	15 mL
¼ cup	50 mL
⅓ cup	75 mL
½ cup	125 mL
¾ cup	175 mL
1 cup	250 mL
1 pt.	500 mL
1 quart	1 L
4 oz.	115 g
8 oz.	225 g
1 lb.	450 g

KITCHEN AND BAKING TIPS

1. To keep dates from sticking when you cut them, oil your knife or scissors.
2. To measure honey or maple syrup, first measure the oil for the recipe in the same cup, or oil the cup before measuring. The sweetener will slip out easily.
3. To prevent bread dough from sticking to a baking pan, lightly oil the inside bottom and sides of the pan. Make sure the oil does not run. If necessary, lightly wipe out excess with paper towelling. Then shake flour all around the inside of the pan, shake out the excess and tap the pan lightly so that only a thin coating remains. For yeast breads, shape the dough outside of the pan and place it in the oiled and floured pan to rise. For quick breads, scoop the batter into the pan and spread evenly. Loosen the bread with a table knife 10–15 minutes after baking, and it will slide from the pan easily.
4. To keep cakes from sticking to the pan, use the method described above for breads. *Or*, oil the bottom of the pan, line it with waxed paper and oil the waxed paper. After baking, loosen the sides of the cake with a table knife, turn the cake upside-down on a rack and peel off the waxed paper.
5. When baking, make sure baking pans are at least 1 inch from each other and from the sides of the oven. If two racks are used, do not place one pan directly above the other.
6. To avoid fallen cakes and quick breads, try not to open the oven door or jostle the pan until the cake or bread is nearly done.
7. To test a cake or a quick bread (baking powder bread) for doneness, insert a toothpick into the middle of the cake. It will come out clean when the cake is done. A cake or bread may look completely baked in the oven, but it may still be raw inside. Be sure not to remove the cake from the oven while testing, or it will stop baking and remain uncooked inside — even with further baking time!
8. For maximum flavour, serve freshly baked cakes and breads at room temperature.

IMPORTANT TIPS ON BAKING BREADS

1. Egg-free and yeast-free baking powder breads rise a bit better and hold together better with 1–1½ tsp. guar gum added as a binder. Avoid using guar gum with yeasted breads, however, as it can hinder rising. Eggs and liquid lecithin are good binders but can be omitted entirely for certain diets if 2 tsp. guar gum is used. A powdered egg substitute can also be purchased to replace eggs in many bread and cake recipes. Make sure to add ¼ cup extra liquid for *each* omitted egg.

2. Breads bake more easily in metal pans and they burn more easily in glass ones. If glass pans must be used, lower the baking temperature 10–25 degrees and watch carefully during baking. Avoid stick-free pans for gluten-free breads. They tend to burn baked goods around the edges, while leaving the middle undercooked.

3. Salt is very important to the flavour of most breads. If you must leave it out, add a bit of cinnamon, allspice or a smaller amount of potassium chloride to enhance the flavour.

4. Some breads made mainly with rice flours and all breads made with millet flour may be a bit bitter or acidic in flavour if ingredients are not properly balanced. They also tend to become bitter when refrigerated. Cool these breads to room temperature, and store whatever bread you can eat in one day in a tin or breadbox. Then slice and freeze the leftovers, to be used piece by piece later. Other flours like buckwheat counteract the bitterness. Buckwheat-Millet Bread (page 108), for example, keeps well for several days in the refrigerator. Apple-Millet Bread (page 119) is best if eaten or frozen within 24 hours. Cinnamon, spices, milk substitutes, sweeteners and fruit juices also help counteract bitterness in baked goods using rice flour and millet flour.

5. For best results, oil baking pans and lightly flour with tapioca flour, which is mildly sweet. Buckwheat flour and arrowroot powder also work well for flouring pans.

6. Breads can be topped with poppy or sesame seeds for added appeal. Sprinkle lightly on top of baking powder breads just before baking. Press lightly into the top of yeast breads while shaping and before putting in a pan to rise.
7. Most of the quick bread (baking powder bread) batters can be made into muffins as well. A recipe for one loaf makes about 18 (1½ dozen) muffins. Lightly oil and flour the muffin cups, then fill ⅔ to ¾ full with batter, and bake 20–40 minutes at 350°F–375°F, or the same temperature the quick bread recipe indicates. Fill any leftover empty muffin cups with water before baking.
8. See the Food Glossary (page 162) for special tips about each baking ingredient.

HOMEMADE FLOURS

1–2 cups legumes (brown or red lentils, green or yellow split peas)
or
1–2 cups whole grains (brown rice, sweet brown rice, quinoa, millet, buckwheat, kasha)
or
1–2 cups nuts or seeds (almonds, cashews, filberts, Brazil nuts, walnuts, pecans, pistachios, sunflower seeds, sesame seeds, pumpkin seeds)
or
1–2 cups dried vegetables (carrots, peppers, potatoes, peas, celery, parsnips, zucchini, squash)*

Sort the legumes, whole grains, or nuts and remove any broken, discoloured or spoiled ones. If using a blender, grind the food, ¼ cup at a time, into powder. If using a food processor, you may grind ½-1 cup at a time. Grind the food as finely as possible, then sift it several times to ensure fineness. Whatever does not pass through the sifter, return to the grinding device. Grind again and sift again. Repeat until everything is ground as fine as possible into a flour.

Use these homemade flours in recipes with other purchased flours like tapioca or arrowroot. Homemade flours can be too coarse when used alone, and may hinder the binding or rising of baked foods.

*For vegetable flours, try the vegetables suggested and experiment with other vegetables. Use a potato peeler to slice the vegetables in thin strips, or slice paper thin, and spread on a dry, flat oven tray. Bake for 1 hour or more at 200°F until the vegetables are dry and a bit crispy. Let the vegetables cool completely, then grind and sift as directed.

ABOUT BAKING POWDER

Baking powders consist of an acidic ingredient, like cream of tartar, and an alkaline ingredient, like baking soda. These are mixed thoroughly with a starch ingredient, usually white flour. Sometimes other additives are included.

Most supermarket brands of baking powder contain wheat and sometimes corn, plus harmful ingredients such as aluminum (alum) or other additives that can aggravate some allergies. Some health food stores sell different brands of wheat-free baking powders, and some pharmacies sell an allergy baking powder or will custom-make it for you.

The ingredients for the following homemade baking powders can be purchased at most health food stores, supermarkets and pharmacies. See the Food Glossary (page 162) and the Buying Guide (page 177) for more information.

Important: Homemade baking powders do not contain aluminum or other harmful, fast-rising, long-lasting ingredients. Store them in dry, tightly sealed glass jars with metal lids and keep in a cool, dry cupboard. Once the wet and dry ingredients (containing baking powder) of a recipe are mixed together, bake the cake or bread immediately, otherwise the baking powder may lose some or all of its rising "action."

General Instructions for Preparing Your Own Baking Powder

Put a flour sifter in or over a bowl and put the ingredients in the sifter, in the exact order given. After all the ingredients are in the sifter, sift them into the bowl. Re-sift them into another bowl, and continue until you have sifted them 4–5 times and they are thoroughly mixed.

Place the baking powder in a clean, dry glass jar with a metal lid and store in a cool, dry cupboard. Make sure the jar is tightly closed! Prolonged exposure to air can spoil the effectiveness of the powder. Use within 3 months.

Baking Powder #1   E · G · S · Y · Gr

    2 Tbs. baking soda
    4 Tbs. arrowroot powder, potato flour *or*
            tapioca flour
    4 Tbs. cream of tartar

Mix and store as described in general instructions, above.

Baking Powder #2   E · G · S · Y · Gr

    5 Tbs. sodium bicarbonate *or* potassium
            bicarbonate
    8 Tbs. arrowroot powder, potato flour *or*
            tapioca flour
    7 Tbs. calcium phosphate (monobasic)

Mix and store as described in general instructions, above.

Baking Powder #3   E · G · S · Y · Gr

2 Tbs. calcium carbonate
4 Tbs. arrowroot powder, potato flour *or*
     tapioca flour
4 Tbs. cream of tartar

Mix and store as described in general instructions, above.

Low Sodium Baking Powder #1
E · G · S · Y · Gr

2 Tbs. potassium bicarbonate
4 Tbs. arrowroot powder, potato flour *or*
     tapioca flour
4 Tbs. cream of tartar

Mix and store as described in general instructions, above.

Low Sodium Baking Powder #2
E · G · S · Y · Gr

2 Tbs. potassium bicarbonate
5 Tbs. arrowroot powder, potato flour *or*
     tapioca flour
4 Tbs. cream of tartar
2 tsp. tartaric acid

Mix and store as described in general instructions, above.

Good Rise Baking Powder
E · G · S · Y · Gr

2 Tbs. baking soda *or* potassium
     bicarbonate
4 Tbs. arrowroot powder, potato flour *or*
     tapioca flour

4 Tbs. cream of tartar *or* calcium
phosphate (monobasic)
5 Tbs. guar gum

Mix and store as described in general instructions, above. For this baking powder, use 1 ½ times the amount of baking powder called for in a recipe. For example, if the recipe calls for 3 tsp. baking powder, use 4 ½ tsp. of this baking powder.

This good-binding baking powder is especially great in egg-free recipes!

"Add to Recipe" Baking Powders

These baking powders are not mixed separately and then stored for use in recipes. They are individually added to a recipe like any other ingredient. This saves time and trouble in the kitchen by eliminating the need for pre-made baking powders. Use these in place of other leavening called for in an existing recipe, or when making up a new recipe.

For 1 loaf bread or a small cake, use one of the following:

1. 2 Tbs. fresh squeezed lemon juice, added to recipe's *wet* ingredients.
2. 2 Tbs. apple cider vinegar, added to recipe's *wet* ingredients.
3. ¼ tsp. vitamin C crystals, added to recipe's *dry* ingredients. *Note:* These crystals sometimes contain corn. Check the label or ask the supplier to make sure.

Use *one* of the above 3 ingredients *and* 1–1 ½ tsp. baking soda. Add the soda to the recipe's *dry* ingredients.

For 2 loaves bread or a large cake, use one of the following:

1. 3 Tbs. fresh squeezed lemon juice, added to recipe's *wet* ingredients.
2. 3 Tbs. apple cider vinegar, added to recipe's *wet* ingredients.
3. ¼ tsp. vitamin C crystals, added to recipe's *dry* ingredients. *Note:* These crystals sometimes contain corn. Check the label or ask the supplier to make sure.

Use *one* of the above 3 ingredients *and* 1½–2 tsp. baking soda. Add the soda to the recipe's *dry* ingredients.

ABOUT WHOLE GRAINS

Whole grains are delicious, nutritious and more digestible than refined grains when properly prepared. They are less likely to aggravate allergic conditions, low blood sugar, diabetes and candida. They contain natural fibre and are lower in calories than many refined food products.

There are cereal grains (described on page 40) and main dish grains (described on page 86). See the Food Glossary (page 162) for more information on individual whole grains.

Special Tips on Whole Grains

1. Grains are generally cooked in 2 or more cups of water per 1 cup of grain.
2. Cook grains until they are no longer crunchy, but not soggy or mushy. Grains should be tender and easy to chew. Improperly cooked grains are extremely hard to digest!
3. Very few grains need to be soaked before cooking. These include wild rice (sometimes), whole oats, rye and wheat kernels (berries).
4. Raw rolled, flaked or crushed grains must be soaked before eating. Toasted grains may be eaten as they are or with milk

substitutes or fruit juices (apple, pear and peach are excellent for this).

5. Before cooking, check grains for dirt balls, gravel, husks and other foreign particles by spreading them out thinly and fingering through them.

6. Brown rice and quinoa are usually the only grains that need prewashing, but you may wash any grain if you feel it needs it.

7. It makes little difference whether you start cooking a grain in cool or warm water. The exception is ground cereals, which get lumpy when put in warm water, unless mixed in carefully with a wire whisk.

8. To prevent grains from boiling over and to distribute heat evenly, water and grains together should never cover more than three-fourths of the cooking pot.

9. Do not add salt or oil to whole grains until the last 10–15 minutes of cooking, to make digestion easier.

10. Any grain in *whole* form (does not include rolled or broken whole grains) will never burn during its *first* cooking process as long as the water does not run out and the grain does not become overcooked to the point that it falls apart (this usually takes 1 ¼ hours or longer). Also, they must be cooked on low heat.

11. Never stir whole grains while cooking or they will stick and burn.

12. When reheating cooked whole grains, add ¼ – ½ cup extra water per cup of grain. Cook the grain, covered, on very low heat until warmed. Brown rice can be reheated by steaming in a vegetable steamer.

13. One cup of dry whole grain or cereal makes about 4 servings.

14. The main dish grains can almost always be substituted one for the other in different recipes, except for wild rice. Grains are similar, but may differ slightly in taste.

15. Wheat, rye, barley and oats contain gluten. See *gluten* in Food Glossary (page 162), and check the Food Glossary for more information on each individual grain and its uses.

HOW TO COOK BEANS PROPERLY FOR GOOD DIGESTION (And No Gas!)

1. Measure the amount of beans (peas/legumes) required and sort through them and remove any misshapen, discoloured or damaged beans, dirt balls, gravel or other foreign objects.
2. Soak 1 cup of dry beans in 3–4 cups of cool or room temperature water and let the beans soak 8 hours or more uncovered. Soak chick peas 12 hours or more and soak soybeans 24 hours. Avoid using soybeans as they usually require a pressure cooker.
3. *Important:* Throw away the water the beans soaked in. This soaking water contains a gas released by the beans while soaking, which in turn will give you gas.
4. Rinse the beans several times and swish them around in fresh water.
5. Put the beans in a large pot so that beans fill only about half of the pot and add fresh water until the beans are covered by 1″ or so of water.
6. Bring the beans and water, uncovered, to a boil on high heat.
7. When the beans are boiling, a white foam or froth will generally form on top. Scoop this off and discard it. This is part of what contributes to gas.
8. Add extra water if needed so the beans are still at least 1″ under water and turn the heat down to very low, just low enough so the beans are barely bubbling. They cook best at this temperature.
9. *Optional:* Add 1 tsp. ground fennel or preferably 1 tsp. savoury to the beans. This also improves their digestibility.
10. Cook for 1¼ hours or more until the beans are very tender and a bean can easily be mashed with the tongue on the roof of the mouth.
11. Always chew beans slowly, never eat them fast or when under excessive stress or fatigue.
12. Have some raw foods first in a meal before eating the beans, to aid in their digestion.

ABOUT SWEETENERS

The amount of sweetener called for in a recipe may be altered to suit your own taste. If you like less sweetener, add less. A recipe can be made sweeter by reducing the amount of flour by about ½ cup and adding about ½ cup of powdered or granulated sweetener. Maple syrup or other sweetener may be substituted for honey in most recipes.

Fruit juice concentrates may be used in place of honey or maple syrup, in about equal proportions.

Regular fruit juice may be used as a sole sweetening agent in some recipes, with small variations in flavour. For example, if a recipe calls for 2 cups honey and 1½ cups nut milk, use 3½ cups of a thick variety of peach or pear juice (other fruit juices are not as sweet or light-coloured). There will be a slight change in flavour. If a recipe using only fruit juice is not sweet enough, substitute ½ cup or so of one of the recipe's dry ingredients (like flour) with the same amount of a natural powdered or granulated sweetener.

Check the Food Glossary (page 162) for more details on each sweetener listed below.

Alternative Sweeteners

amazake (rice culture
  sweetener)
honey
maple syrup
maple sugar
brown date sugar
molasses
fructose
date spread
fruit sugar (unrefined)
fruit butter

fruit juice
fruit concentrate
fruit juice concentrate
honeyleaf (stevia)
natural raw sugar
  (SUCANAT®)
sorghum
barley malt powder and
  syrup (*Note:* barley
  contains gluten)

ABOUT EGGS: WHITES vs. YOLKS

Some people cannot tolerate egg yolks, but can eat egg whites. In most recipes, 2 stiffly beaten egg whites can be used in place of 1 egg, but don't add them as you would add an egg. Just before baking, after all other ingredients are combined, gently fold in the egg whites and bake as directed.

If you can eat egg yolks but not the whites, you can usually substitute two well-beaten egg yolks for 1 egg in many recipes. Add them as you would a whole egg.

EGG SUBSTITUTES

Liquid lecithin is used in some recipes instead of eggs. It is best if used along with 2 tsp. guar gum. Experiment with lecithin and guar gum in other recipes.

A powdered egg substitute can also be purchased to replace eggs in many bread and cake recipes. It is best to use a bit more egg replacer than the package may suggest. For *each* egg omitted, use 2–3 tsp. powdered egg replacer added to the dry ingredients, and 3 ½ Tbs. water or other liquid added to the wet ingredients.

You can make your own egg substitute to use as a binder, not a leavening agent. Combine ⅓ cup water and 3–4 tsp. brown flax seeds. Bring to a boil on high heat, then simmer on low heat for 5–7 minutes until a slightly thickened gel begins to form. Strain the flax seed out of the liquid and use the gel in recipes. This recipe makes enough substitute for 1 egg. Increase the amounts as needed to substitute for 2, 3 or more eggs. Some people prefer to leave the flax seeds in the mixture after thickening, or blend them into the gel before using. This may alter the recipe's taste a little.

For more information, see Tip #1 about egg-free recipes, in Important Tips on Baking Breads (page 18).

THICKENERS

Cold Foods

For *cold* foods, like salad dressings, ice creams, gelatin substitutes, puddings:

What to use: Guar gum, xanthan gum, other gums.

How to use: Use blender, electric mixer or food processor to mix with other ingredients and they thicken almost instantly.

How much to use: 1–2 tsp. powdered gum per recipe (about 1 loaf of bread, 1 cake or 2 cups liquid).

Hot Foods

For *hot* foods, like gravies, sauces, stews, soups, heated puddings, breads, baked desserts:

What to use: Guar gum, xanthan gum, arrowroot (see below), agar agar powder (see below).

How to use: In *dry* ingredients, mix thoroughly with other ingredients before baking. In *liquids*, mix in cold liquid, heat and stir until thickened. Let cool to set.

How much to use: 1–3 tsp. powdered thickener per recipe (about 1 loaf of bread, 1 cake or up to 1 quart liquid).

Other Thickeners

Agar agar: Use about 1–2 tsp. powder or 2–6 tsp. flakes to thicken 1–2 cups liquid. Mix with cool liquid and heat slowly, stirring, until thickened. Remove from heat, strain and add to recipe.

Arrowroot: Use ½–1 tsp. to thicken 1 cup liquid. Mix with cool liquid and heat slowly, stirring until thickened. Remove from heat or add to recipe.

Kudzu: To use kudzu as a thickener, 1 tsp. kudzu = 3 tsp. flour; 2 tsp. kudzu = 3 tsp. arrowroot.
Use 1–2 tsp. kudzu to thicken 1 cup soup or sauce.
Use 1–2 Tbs. kudzu per cup to make jello or jelled desserts.
Crush the powdered chunks in cold liquid, mash and dissolve well. Strain and heat to thicken.

See the Food Glossary (page 162) for more information on agar agar, arrowroot, guar gum, kudzu and xanthan gum.

CLARIFIED BUTTER, AN OIL SUBSTITUTE

Most people allergic to dairy products are unable to enjoy butter, but many can tolerate clarified butter. It adds flavour to many dishes, and when liquid or softened, it can be used in place of oil in many main dishes and cookies.

Heat 1 lb. butter in a heavy saucepan on very low heat for 1 hour until the butter is melted and has separated. Skim off the foamy white milk solids from the top of the liquid. Save the yellow liquid below it, but be careful *not* to include the whey and milk solids on the bottom of the pan. Store in a covered container and refrigerate. It stays fresh for many weeks.

ABOUT TOFU

Tofu is a wonderful meat or dairy substitute made from soy. It is low in calories and contains no cholesterol. 8 oz. (about 225 gm) of tofu provides: 164 calories, 17.6 gm protein, 292 mg calcium (the same as 8 oz. milk), 286 mg phosphorus, 96 mg potassium and as much iron as 4–5 eggs.

Although tofu is bland by itself, it works wonders in recipes as it absorbs the flavours of the ingredients around it and actually extends and complements the taste of sauces, gravies, herbs and spices. Used correctly, tofu is delicious and adds texture, protein and other nutrients to all types of dishes, including salads, main dishes, dressings, sauces and desserts.

Store tofu completely covered by fresh water, preferably in a glass jar, in the refrigerator. Plain tofu is fresh as long as it retains its milky white colour and has no scent or taste. If the tofu smells a bit, rinse it thoroughly. If no smell remains, it can still be cooked but should not be eaten "raw." If the tofu still has an odour *after* rinsing – discard it!

Whenever the freshness of tofu is questionable or to avoid any chance of bacteria growth, lightly steam it for 4–9 minutes before using it.

Soft, pressed and regular tofu are available. The soft tofu may be used in any dessert recipe for a less grainy texture. However, regular tofu may be used unless specified otherwise.

ABOUT MILK SUBSTITUTES

For many people, milk substitutes are an acquired taste. If you are only recently off dairy milk, give yourself some time to get acquainted with these special and lovely flavours. You may find you want to drink them once or twice a day, but you can also enjoy them just a few times a week. Other foods like nuts, seeds, tofu, whole grains and vegetables will supply the nutrients you need to replace milk. Cashews, almonds and sesame seeds add lots of calcium and protein to dairy-free diets.

Cashew Milk #1 (Plain)
E · G · S · Y · B · Gr

Use this version for bread and cake recipes, unless otherwise specified.

  2 cups water
  2–3 Tbs. raw cashew pieces

Blend ingredients thoroughly in a blender for several minutes until the water becomes white. Strain and stir well before using. Keeps several days in the refrigerator, or may be frozen for later use.

Note: Technically speaking, all cashews must be slightly cooked before being sold. Buy the ones called "raw" in the store.

Cashew Milk #2   E · G · S · Y · B · Gr

Use this version as a beverage, or when specified in recipes.

> 1 cup raw cashew pieces
> 1 cup water
> 2 Tbs. honey *or* 1 ½ Tbs. maple syrup
> 2 Tbs. lecithin granules
> 2 Tbs. light, cold-pressed oil
>
> 3 cups water

Combine all ingredients *except* the 3 cups water in a blender. Blend thoroughly. Slowly add the 3 cups water and blend again. Stir before each use. Do not strain.

Almond Milk #1 and #2
E · G · S · Y · B · Gr

Follow the directions for Cashew Milk #1 or #2, but use *blanched*, chopped almonds in place of cashews. Almond milk can be used instead of cashew milk in any recipe.

Sesame or Sunflower Milk
E · G · S · Y · B · Gr

> 1 cup cold water
> ⅓ cup hulled or unhulled sesame seeds *or*
>   ⅓ – ½ cup hulled sunflower seeds

Optional: 1–2 tsp. honey *or* maple syrup *or*
3–4 pitted dates

Blend the cold water and seeds on high speed in a blender for 1–2 minutes. Strain twice through a fine strainer or cheese-cloth. Sweetener may be added after straining, if desired. Do not use sweetener if milk is to be used in baking recipes.

Plain Soy Milk   E · G · Y · B · Gr

Use this soy milk for bread and basic recipes.
    2 cups water
    5–6 Tbs. instant soy milk powder

Blend ingredients well and stir before each use. Keeps a few days in the refrigerator, or may be frozen for later use.

Sweet Soy Milk   E · G · Y · B · Gr

Drink this soy milk just as it is, or use it in beverages and dessert recipes.
    2 cups water
    5–6 Tbs. instant soy milk powder
    ½ tsp. real vanilla flavouring*
    1–2 Tbs. honey, maple syrup, barley malt
            powder, barley malt syrup *or*
            4–6 pitted dates

Blend ingredients well and stir before each use. Keeps a few days in the refrigerator. *Add a few drops of maple, butter-scotch, nut or mint flavouring with or instead of the vanilla, if desired.

About Coconut Milks

Most coconut milk powders contain whey and other milk solids, so they should be avoided by people with dairy allergies.

However, most bottled liquid coconut juices are pure. These can be used carefully in *some* recipes, but must be experimented with, as they can change the flavour and consistency of a dish. If you find a pure coconut milk powder, blend it with water until it reaches the desired consistency. Add flavourings as desired.

Preparing Fresh Coconut

Make sure the woody outer husk of the coconut has been removed to reveal the brown, stringy, oblong shelled inner coconut. Usually this outer husk is removed before the coconut is sold in a store. If not, the husk looks like it has been chopped off like wood in rough, uneven strokes.

Hold the whole coconut in one hand, about 6" above a large bowl. Take a hammer in your other hand and give the coconut a good whack. After 2–4 good whacks, the coconut should crack and dispense its juice into the bowl. Another whack or two should break the coconut in half and open it up so the white fleshy pulp can be removed. Use a *round*-edged table knife to cut and pry the coconut flesh from the shell. *Do not* use a sharp, pointed knife, as many knife-tips have been broken off and lodged dangerously in the coconut flesh, not to mention the loss of a good knife! The white pulp will retain a very thin brown skin on the inner side. This skin is edible, or it may be peeled off if desired. If the coconut shell has cracked nicely, the pieces make pretty, waterproof planters.

Drink the coconut milk (juice) fresh or use it in recipes. It keeps about 2–3 days refrigerated. Eat the fresh coconut pieces right away or store them in a glass jar, refrigerate and eat within 5 days. You may also blend small pieces of fresh coconut (peel off the brown "skin" first) with water, according to personal taste, to make a thick coconut milk for drinking or using in recipes. Fresh coconut can also be shredded and/or dried for later use. It is best if not frozen.

Coconut Milk   E · G · S · Y · B · Gr

1 cup water
¼ – ½ cup shredded unsweetened coconut

Blend ingredients thoroughly and strain if needed. Coconut milk adds a coconut flavour to recipes. Add extra sweetening if desired.

Zucchini Milk   E · G · S · Y · B · Gr

1 cup finely grated zucchini
      water

Choose firm, bright green and white coloured zucchini. The dark or yellowish ones are bitter. Peel zucchini if desired. Blend the grated zucchini in the blender with just enough water to keep the blades turning, and create a thick, white "milk." Strain if desired. Use with or without sweetening in recipes.

Alfalfa Milk   E · G · S · Y · B · Gr

1 cup alfalfa sprouts
      water

Rinse the sprouts thoroughly to remove all brown hulls, or cut off the brown seed hulls if necessary. Blend the sprouts in the blender with just enough water to keep the blades turning, and create a "milk." Strain if desired. Use with or without sweetening in recipes.

BEVERAGES

Carob Milk   E · G · Y · B · Gr · can be S

2 cups *plain, unsweetened* soy milk,
            cashew milk *or* almond milk
2–3 Tbs. honey *or* maple syrup, *or* 4–8
            pitted dates, blended
⅛–½ tsp. real vanilla, maple, nut, mint, rum
            or other flavouring
4–6 tsp. carob powder

Blend ingredients well and serve chilled and stirred. Add 1–2
of the flavourings. Use within 1–2 days.

Carob Malted   E · Y · B · Gr · can be S

Follow the directions for Carob Milk, above, using the full 6
tsp. carob powder. Add 3 Tbs. barley malt powder or syrup.
Optional flavour enhancers are 1 tsp. light oil and a few dashes
of sea salt. Blend very well, chill and serve. Use within 1–2
days. Add 1 whole banana, fresh or frozen, for added flavour
if desired.

Carob Shake   G · Y · B · Gr · can be E · S

Follow the directions for Carob Milk, above, using the full 6
tsp. carob powder. Blend well. Add 1 scoop natural dairy-free
ice cream (page 152) and blend lightly. Serve immediately.

Carrot Shake   G · Y · B · Gr · can be E · S

6 oz. carrot juice (fresh preferably)
1 scoop dairy-free vanilla ice cream (see
page 152)

Blend both ingredients lightly in a blender and serve immediately. A nicely sweet, delicious and nutritious beverage. Extra liquid sweetening may be added if desired.

Hot Carob Milk   Y · B · Gr · can be E · G · S

Follow the directions for Carob Milk or Carob Malted, above (without added banana), and add a few drops of rum or butterscotch flavouring if desired. Heat on medium heat, simmer 1 minute or more, while stirring, until hot. Serve immediately with a cinnamon stir stick or a sprinkle of cinnamon. Delicious!

Tofu Fruit Smoothie   E · G · Y · B · Gr

2 cups fresh strawberries (about 1 small
basket)*
2 large bananas*
4 oz. tofu
⅛–¼ cup liquid sweetener
2–3 tsp. real vanilla flavouring

water or fruit juice

Blend all ingredients thoroughly, adding just enough water or fruit juice to bring the smoothie to the desired consistency. Serve immediately.

*The strawberries or bananas should be frozen before the smoothie is prepared, to ensure it is very cool after blending. Instead of these fruits, you may use one or two of the following: blueberries, raspberries, peaches, pears, apricots, kiwi, mangos or others. You may also add dates or other dried fruit to help sweeten the drink, along with nut milks or other milks.

Natural Cool-Aid   E · G · S · Y · B · Gr

> 1 cup water
> ¼ cup fruit juice (preferably: grape, pear, peach, apple, raspberry or other berry juice)

Use 100% real fruit juice in this recipe. Use cold water in the recipe or chill before serving. Stir the liquids together. Additional sweetening may be added but is rarely required.

Natural Pop #1   E · G · S · Y · B · Gr

> ½ cup club soda or sparkling mineral water
> ½ cup fruit juice (preferably: grape, pear, peach, apple, raspberry or other berry juice)

Mix chilled ingredients together well and serve.
   Note: Club soda tends to loosen the bowels, while sparkling mineral water tends to contribute to constipation for some individuals.

Natural Pop #2   E · G · S · Y · B · Gr

> 1 cup club soda or sparkling mineral water
> 1–3 Tbs. orange, pineapple, apple or other fresh or frozen fruit juice concentrate

Follow the directions for Natural Pop #1, above.

Fruit Slushes   E · G · S · Y · B · Gr

1 cup fruit juice
4–5 ice cubes
Optional: 1–2 tsp. sweetener (or to taste)

Blend all ingredients in a blender until the ice is chopped fine.

Lemonade   E · G · S · Y · B · Gr

slightly less than 1 qt. water
juice of 2–3 large lemons
3–4 Tbs. liquid sweetener
ice cubes

Heat 1 cup of the water until very hot. Mix the sweetener into the hot water until dissolved. Add the remaining cold water and lemon juice, then add enough ice cubes to make 1 qt. lemonade. If ice is not available, use a full 1 qt. water and chill the lemonade before serving.

Pink Lemonade   E · G · S · Y · B · Gr

Follow the directions for Lemonade (above), and blend in ½–1 cup fresh or frozen strawberries. Add a bit more sweetening if needed.

Nectar of the Gods   E · G · S · Y · B · Gr

1 qt. lemonade
1 qt. pineapple juice
1–2 cups strawberries*

Blend all ingredients together and chill or serve with ice.
    *Instead of the strawberries, you may use sweet cherries, sweetened cranberry juice or blended, strained raspberries.

BREAKFASTS

PREPARING CEREAL GRAINS

Make sure to read About Whole Grains (page 24).

Raw Cereals

Flaked whole-grain cereals such as flaked oats, rye, wheat (if you can eat it), rice, barley and millet are not always available. Prepare and serve them like soaked organic rolled oats (below), or toast them in the oven like granola and serve with milk substitute and flavourings.

Granola and other toasted grain cereals are made with toasted rolled oats or other rolled grain, nuts and seeds, dried fruit, sweetening, etc. Serve with milk substitute or fruit juice, or eat them right out of the package. Chew them well.

Muesli and other raw cereals are usually made with rolled, cracked or flaked whole grains, ground or chopped nuts and seeds, and sometimes shredded coconut, raisins or other dried fruits. If the cereal is organic or contains very tough, fibrous grains, prepare it the same way as soaked organic rolled oats (above). If the cereal is just natural and less fibrous, prepare it the same way as soaked natural rolled oats (below).

Natural rolled oats (regular or old-fashioned) Soak 1 cup oats in 1 cup of very warm water for 10–15 minutes. Add flavourings and/or cut fruit, and serve.

Organic rolled oats are smaller and rounder than natural rolled oats and must be soaked for several hours or overnight before eating, unless they are "crushed" or chopped after rolling, then they soak or cook as easily as natural oats. These are usually found only in health food stores and are almost always labelled "organic." After soaking in 1–1½ cups water per 1 cup of oats, drain off excess water (if any) and serve with sweetening, milk substitute and/or fruit.

Rolled rice or barley can be used in place of oats in recipes.

Puffed whole-grain cereals include puffed amaranth, oats, corn, rice, millet, wheat (if you can eat it) and others. They are usually unsweetened. Serve them as they are with milk substitute and sweetening as desired.

Cooked Cereals

Amaranth. Although amaranth grain can be cooked as a breakfast cereal, it is not that tasty. It is better to use the flour in recipes or buy the puffed amaranth cereal available in many health food stores. Notice that it is usually added to a cereal rather than sold by itself as a cereal. If desired, cook it in 2 times as much water for a rice-like texture, and 2½–3 times as much water for cereal or to add to breads. Cook until tender, about 18–20 minutes.

Cornmeal. Use 2–2½ cups water per 1 cup cornmeal. The coarser the meal, the more water is needed and the longer the cooking time. Start water and cornmeal cooking together in cool or lukewarm water and stir together on medium heat. Use a wire whisk to make sure the cereal does not become lumpy. After 1–2 minutes, the cereal must be stirred constantly for 10 minutes or more until it is no longer grainy. Add extra water if needed. Cornmeal should always have a sweetener like honey added to it. Raisins, dates, or coconut and cinnamon cooked into the cereal are also very delicious. Sea salt is optional. Store dry cornmeal in a cool place or in the freezer, but never refrigerate it or it will have a damp, musty flavour.

Quinoa (pronounced "keen-wah"). Rinse thoroughly before cooking by rubbing the grains together well in a pot of water and changing the water 2–4 times. This helps to remove the saponin, which may irritate digestion or allergies. Cook like millet (see below), but use 2–3 cups water to 1 cup quinoa and cook 20–35 minutes until tender.

Millet (cereal). Use 3–4 cups of water per 1 cup millet. (More water is used for the cereal than for main dish millet.) Bring water and millet to a boil. Dates can be added now if desired — delicious! Use ¼ – ½ cup dates per 1 cup millet. Then turn down heat and simmer, covered, for 50–60 minutes until the millet breaks down and is very soft and mushlike. Before serving, stir the cereal to mix in the dates. Serve with milk substitute or juice and oil and also honey, if no dates are added. Add sea salt if desired.

Cooked oatmeal. *Whole rolled natural oatmeal and chopped rolled organic oatmeal* (regular or old-fashioned): Use 1–1½ cups water per 1 cup natural rolled oats. Bring water to a boil and add oats. Stir once, cover and remove from heat. Let sit for 10–15 minutes before serving. Add flavourings to taste. Another method for these types of oats is the soaked oats method: Put the oats in a sturdy bowl and pour very hot or boiling water over them. Cover and let sit 10–15 minutes. Do not stir! Add flavourings or stewed or fresh fruit and enjoy. This method preserves more of the beneficial enzymes found in oats, and many people feel the oats taste better because they do not get gummy or sticky.

Whole rolled organic oatmeal. Use 1½–2 cups water per 1 cup organic rolled oats. Bring the water to a boil, then turn down heat and add oats. Stir constantly and cook for 5–10 minutes or until oats are easy to chew. Then turn off heat, cover oatmeal and let it sit for 10–15 minutes before serving. Add flavourings to taste.

Whole oats and whole spelt. Cook as for main dish oats (page 40). Serve plain with sea salt, with oil and honey or with maple syrup.

Sweet rice. Cook and serve like millet cereal (above), but use 2–3 cups water per 1 cup rice and cook it for 50–60 minutes until tender.

Teff. Bring ½ cup teff seed and 2 cups of water to a boil, then turn down heat and simmer for 15–20 minutes or until all the water is absorbed. Cook ¼ cup raisins, currants or dates with the teff if desired. If dried fruit is not used, serve the cereal with maple syrup, fruit concentrate or other sweetener and a bit of sea salt or cinnamon.

Granola #1   E · S · Y · B · can be G

6–8 cups rolled oats, rolled rice *or* rolled
          barley
4–6 cups mixed nuts, seeds and chopped
          dried fruit
½–⅔ cup light, cold-pressed oil
1–1½ cups honey *or* maple syrup
1 tsp. sea salt

Mix together the grains, nuts and seeds, but set aside the dried fruit. In a separate large bowl, combine the oil, sweetener and salt. Add the dry mixture to the wet and mix together with a large wooden spoon or with your hands.

Preheat the oven to 350°F. Lightly oil two flat baking pans or pizza pans and spread the granola mixture on them about ½–⅔″ deep. Bake for 12–18 minutes until the top layer is browned. Then remove the granola from the oven, stir or turn all the granola and replace it in the oven. Bake for another 4–5 minutes until the top is browned, then remove and stir again. Bake the granola for a final 4–5 minutes and remove it from the oven into a large bowl. The mixture will be moist, but it will dry up and harden as it cools. Mix in the dried fruit now (it will burn if placed in the oven with the granola).

Let the granola cool before storing. Break it up every 10 minutes or so to keep it from hardening into one lump as it cools. When cool, store covered in refrigerator or in a cool, dry place.

Granola is quite tasty just as it is for a snack or breakfast cereal. It can be served with milk substitute, apple juice or applesauce poured on the cereal.

Granola #2   E · S · Y · B · can be G

6 cups	rolled oats, rolled rice *or* rolled barley
1 cup	sunflower seeds
1–2 cups	chopped almonds, cashews, filberts (hazelnuts), walnuts, *or* any combination
½ cup	sesame seeds
½ cup	flax seeds
1 cup	raisins *or* currants
Optional:	1–2 Tbs. unsweetened carob powder
Optional:	1–2 tsp. cinnamon
Optional:	½ cup chopped dates
½–⅔ cup	light, cold-pressed oil (use more, if more honey is used)
1–1½ cups	honey *or* ¾–1 cup maple syrup
1 tsp.	sea salt

Follow the directions for Granola #1, above.

Muesli   E · S · Y · B · can be G

4 cups rolled oats, rolled rice *or* rolled
        barley
1 cup slivered almonds *or* chopped
       walnuts
¼ cup sesame seeds, ground
¼ cup flax seeds, ground
½ cup sunflower seeds, ground
2–3 tsp. carob powder *or* ½–1 tsp
      cinnamon
¼ tsp. sea salt

Mix all ingredients together and refrigerate or keep in a cool, dry place. When ready to eat, prepare this cereal like natural soaked oats or organic soaked oats (page 41), depending on the type of rolled grain used, *or* soak ½ cup cereal in ½–¾ cup very hot water for 15–20 minutes. Then serve with honey and milk substitute, or any way you like. This cereal should be soaked before eating or it will be difficult to digest. Do not eat it raw or "dry."

Ground Nuts Toppings
(for Cereals and Other Foods)

Grind nuts or seeds ¼ cup at a time in a blender at high speed, or use a mortar and pestle. Keep jars of ground nuts in the refrigerator for up to 2–3 weeks for sprinkling on cereals and fruit or vegetable salads. They are also good in casseroles and dessert recipes. Nuts can also be ground in a food processor with the metal blade or, in a pinch, double-bagged and smashed with a hammer!

Brown Rice Breakfast Chews
E · G · S · Y · B

1 cup cooked brown rice, cold
1 Tbs. maple syrup
¼ cup chopped almonds *or* other nuts or
      seeds
¼ cup raisins *or* currants*
¼ cup tapioca flour
1–2 Tbs. arrowroot powder

To prepare the 1 cup brown rice, use about ½ cup uncooked rice. Be sure to measure after cooking, however, as some rice varieties expand more.

Preheat the oven to 300°F. With a fork, mix the cooked rice with the other ingredients, being careful not to mash or crush the rice. When all the flour and arrowroot powder are fully mixed in, drop by heaping teaspoonfuls onto lightly oiled cookie sheets, about 1½–2 inches apart. Flatten the balls to a thickness of ⅜"–½" and bake for 40–50 minutes until firm and lightly browned. Cool for 1 hour and then store in a tin for 1–2 days at room temperature, or 3–7 days in the refrigerator.

*Instead of raisins or currants, you may use chopped dates, dried apricots, dried apples, or extra seeds or chopped nuts.

A simple, satisfying snack for breakfasts on the run or afternoon nibbles. Makes 18–20 chews.

Tips on Pancakes and French Toast

1. Sea salt and cinnamon are optional, but they add to the flavour. Add ¼ tsp. cinnamon to pancakes if desired.
2. ¼–1 tsp. baking powder or 2–3 tsp. arrowroot powder may be added to any of these pancake recipes for thickening.
3. 1–2 Tbs. honey, maple syrup or another sweetener may be added to the pancakes in place of the same amount of other liquid, *except* in the Amazing Amaranth Pancakes.

4. A bit more liquid or flour can be added to a pancake batter if thinner or thicker pancakes are preferred.
5. Pancakes or "toast" can be kept warm in a hot, covered casserole dish in a low heated oven.
6. You may add 1–2 Tbs. soy or amaranth flour to pancakes containing milk substitutes, to add protein to the pancakes. Make sure to reduce another flour by the same amount.
7. Cold French Toast can be reheated in an oven or toaster oven on a low temperature toasting setting.
8. Cold pancakes can be reheated in a covered dish in an oven heated to 350–400°F, for 10 minutes or until hot.
9. Serve hot pancakes and French Toast with Fruit Butter or other syrup blends and toppings (see page 53).

Amazing Amaranth Pancakes
G · S · Y · Gr

1 large or extra large egg, beaten
¼ cup apple juice*
1 tsp. light, cold-pressed oil

¼ cup amaranth flour
¼ cup tapioca flour
3 Tbs. arrowroot powder
¼ tsp. cinnamon
¼ tsp. baking powder (wheat-free)
⅛ tsp. sea salt

Beat the egg until light and foamy. Beat in juice and oil.

Lightly oil a frying pan and heat it until very hot. Lower the heat to medium-high.

While the pan heats, add the remaining ingredients to the egg mixture, one by one, and beat thoroughly after each addition. Once the batter is ready, make pancakes immediately.

Pour 2–3 Tbs. batter into the pan for each pancake, and keep the pan hot. Flip each pancake when it is brown on the bottom.

Watch carefully, as the pancakes cook quickly. Before cooking each new batch, lightly re-oil the pan with a paper towel dipped in oil.

*Instead of apple juice, you may use another sweet fruit juice, such as mango, papaya, peach, pear or apricot.

Makes 8–10 grain-free pancakes, 3″ in diameter.

Millet and/or Rice Pancakes

G · S · Y · can be B

1 large egg
1½ cups milk substitute

2 cups flour (millet flour, brown rice flour
or 1 cup of each)
½ cup tapioca flour
several dashes sea salt

Follow the directions for Amazing Amaranth Pancakes, above. To thicken, add ¼ cup extra flour (your choice), and/or ¼ tsp. baking powder.

Makes 1½–2 dozen light, thin, 3″ pancakes.

Buckwheat Pancakes

G · S · Y · can be B

2 large eggs
1–1¼ cups milk substitute*

1½ cups millet flour *or* brown rice flour
¾ cup buckwheat flour
several dashes sea salt
Optional: ¼ tsp. cinnamon

Follow the directions for Amazing Amaranth Pancakes, above.

*Instead of milk substitute, you may use a sweet fruit juice. Try apple, apricot, peach, pear or tropical fruit juice.

Makes 1½–2 dozen 3″ pancakes.

White Wonder Pancakes   G · S · Y · B

1⅓ cups milk substitute (or a bit more)
2 cups brown rice flour*
½ cup tapioca flour
several dashes sea salt
Optional: 2 tsp. arrowroot powder *or* ¼ tsp.
baking powder
2 large egg whites, beaten stiff

Combine all ingredients *except* egg whites. With a spoon, slowly and gently stir the stiff egg whites into the batter. Make the pancakes immediately, following the directions for Amazing Amaranth Pancakes (page 47).

*Instead of brown rice flour, you may use millet flour, *or* 1 cup brown rice flour and 1 cup millet flour. The pancakes won't be white, but they will still taste great.

Spelt Pancakes   Y · can be S

1 cup spelt flour
½ cup nut milk, seed milk *or* soy milk
1 large egg
2–3 tsp. light, cold-pressed oil
1–2 tsp. liquid sweetener
½ tsp. baking powder
½ tsp. sea salt
Optional: ⅛–¼ tsp. cinnamon

Follow the directions for Amazing Amaranth Pancakes (page 47).

Kamut Pancakes   Y · can be S

Follow the directions for Spelt Pancakes, above, but use 1 cup kamut flour in place of the spelt flour, and use ¾ cup milk substitute in place of the ½ cup nut milk.

Spelt Pancakes Without Eggs

E · Y · can be S

1 cup spelt flour
¾ cup milk substitute
4 tsp. light, cold-pressed oil
1–2 tsp. liquid sweetener
2 tsp. baking powder
½ tsp. sea salt
Optional: ⅛–¼ tsp. cinnamon

Follow the directions for Amazing Amaranth Pancakes (page 47), but omit the egg.

Kamut Pancakes Without Eggs

E · Y · can be S

Follow the directions for Spelt Pancakes Without Eggs, above, but use 1 cup kamut flour in place of the spelt flour and increase the milk substitute to 1 cup.

Amaranth, Buckwheat, Quinoa, Teff or Millet Pancakes Without Eggs

E · G · Y · can be S and/or Gr

Wet ingredients:
6–7 Tbs. apple, pear *or* peach juice
2 tsp. light, cold-pressed oil

Dry ingredients:
¼ cup flour (amaranth, buckwheat,
quinoa, teff *or* millet)
¼ cup tapioca flour *or* brown rice flour
3 Tbs. arrowroot powder
2 tsp. baking powder
⅛ tsp. sea salt

Mix the wet ingredients together. In a separate bowl, mix the dry ingredients together. Avoid using cinnamon in this recipe, as it may hinder rising.

Oil a frying pan and bring quickly to medium heat. Add the dry ingredients to the wet and mix well. Start making the pancakes immediately after the batter is mixed. Cook for about 1 minute until the edges dry up a bit. (Watch the heat, or the pancakes will cook too fast and burn.) Turn over and cook another 15–30 seconds. Do not flatten pancakes when turning them! Turn again to check for readiness, then flatten if desired. Re-oil the frying pan generously before starting each new batch.

Enjoy these great pancakes with all your favourite toppings (see page 53).

Pancake Sandwiches

Cold pancakes make wonderful "breads" for sandwiches. They hold together well and are flavourful and fun, especially for children's lunches!

French Toast

6–8	slices egg-based bread (try Rice Bread, page 106 or Millet Bread, page 107)
2	eggs, well beaten
dash	sea salt
Optional:	1–2 tsp. water

Choose a hearty, firm, homemade bread made with eggs so that it holds together well while being dipped in egg and cooked.

Beat the eggs until they are light and foamy. Add the salt (and water, if desired). Lightly oil a frying pan and heat it until very hot. Lower the heat to medium-high, dip the bread in the egg mixture and place the slices in the hot pan. When the bottom is nicely browned, turn the toast over and brown the other side.

Serve immediately with your favourite syrup blends and toppings (see page 53).

Tofu French Toast

G · Y · B · can be E · Gr
(depending on type of bread used)

Dipping mixture:
7–8 oz. tofu, crumbled
¾ cup milk, soy milk, nut milk *or* water
1–2 Tbs. light, cold-pressed oil
3–4 tsp. liquid sweetener
1 tsp. vanilla extract
½ tsp. cinnamon
several dashes sea salt

bread

maple syrup *or* other liquid
  sweetener
sliced, puréed or stewed fruit
jam
chopped nuts and/or seeds
shredded unsweetened coconut

Blend all Dipping Mixture ingredients together in a blender or food processor. Heat a well-oiled frying pan on medium-high heat. Dip the bread in the tofu mixture and place several slices in the hot pan. Cook a few minutes on each side until lightly browned. Make sure to re-oil the pan before cooking each batch.

Serve with maple syrup, fruit or jam, and top with nuts or coconut if desired.

Syrup Blends and Toppings for Pancakes and French Toast

1. Serve your favourite liquid honey, at room temperature or warmed.
2. Serve maple syrup hot, cold or at room temperature.
3. Mix ½ cup honey and ½ cup maple syrup and serve warm.
4. Blend 1 cup fresh or frozen unsweetened berries with ½–1 cup honey, maple syrup, barley malt syrup or fruit concentrate.
5. Blend fresh bananas, peaches, mangos or other sweet fruits with a little juice and serve hot or cold as a fruit syrup.
6. Serve homemade or store-bought applesauce or jam.
7. Top with fresh sliced fruit or mixed fruit salad.
8. Sprinkle with barley malt powder, maple sugar, natural raw sugar *or* chopped or ground nuts or seeds *or* shredded unsweetened coconut.
9. Top with Date Spread or Fruit Butter (page 157).
10. Top with Carob Fudge Topping or Carob Syrup (page 155).

Emile's Tofu Breakfast Treat

E · G · B · Gr

3 Tbs. nutritional yeast
1 Tbs. olive oil *or* other oil
1 tsp. tamari soy sauce (wheat-free)
¼–¾ tsp. onion powder
several dashes cayenne pepper and sea kelp
Optional: ground nuts or seeds, for garnish

3–4 slices regular tofu, ¼"–⅓" thick

Preheat the oven to 350°F. Thoroughly mix all the ingredients *except* the tofu. Place the tofu slices in a small, unoiled iron skillet or tin pan and spread the tamari-yeast mixture like jam on each piece. Bake for 15–20 minutes or until tender and juicy. Sprinkle with ground nuts or seeds if desired, and eat it hot.

Enjoy this different, delicious breakfast as a nice change. Make a fresh batch each time. Makes 1 serving.

SALADS

PEOPLE WITH SEVERE FOOD ALLERGIES or intolerances often find lettuce, especially iceberg lettuce, very hard to digest, therefore spinach is a more nutritious, digestible choice. Eliminate or substitute any other ingredients that cannot be tolerated, for ingredients of your choice that are as similar as possible. For example, zucchini is generally easier to digest than cucumber, while red bell pepper is better than green. Tomatoes, potatoes and eggplant are members of the deadly nightshade family and are slightly toxic. Some people find them difficult to digest, whether raw or cooked.

Chew all salads very, very well to ensure the best digestion. Those who have difficulty eating salads should include them in the midday meal, rather than with supper or later in the day. If possible, eat some raw vegetables every day, but avoid eating more than 5–7 different raw vegetables at a single meal. Those unable to tolerate raw vegetables should eat several servings of steamed, sautéed, broiled and/or baked vegetables each day.

Buy fresh organic vegetables whenever possible, as pesticides and other chemicals on some vegetables may irritate allergies.

Hard vegetables like carrots and beets should not be peeled but should be cleaned with a strong vegetable scrub brush before using in recipes.

To prepare spinach for salad recipes, wash it well by swishing it in cold water to remove the sand. Remove the stems and dry the leaves, being careful not to twist or bruise them. Tear the spinach into bite-sized pieces.

Spinach Salad   E · G · S · Y · B · Gr

1 small or medium bunch spinach
1 medium zucchini, sliced in rounds
    or half rounds
1 large avocado, cut in thin wedges
    or chunks
1 large carrot *or* medium beet, grated
Optional: 1–2 Tbs. sunflower seeds,
    pre-soaked in water for ½–1
    hour and drained, *or* sliced
    almonds or other nuts, unsoaked

Combine all the ingredients and toss together lightly.
Makes 2–4 servings.

Zucchini Salad   E · G · S · Y · B · Gr

1–2 small zucchini, grated
½ cucumber *or* ¼ English cucumber,
    cut in rounds or half rounds
8–12 red radishes *or* 1–2 carrots, sliced
    into paper-thin rounds
1 green *or* red bell pepper, cut in ¼"
    strips
1–2 leaves romaine, leaf lettuce, red
    lettuce *or* spinach, torn
Optional: 1–2 cauliflower florets, grated
Optional: 1–2 tomatoes, cut in chunks

Combine all the ingredients and toss together lightly.
    Grated zucchini makes a great substitute for lettuce in many
salad recipes. It adds texture and flavour and is easier to digest!
This lovely salad is surprisingly light and delicious. It is
especially nice when served with a creamy dressing. This
recipe makes 2–4 servings.

Sprout Salad Special

E · G · S · Y · B · Gr

1 cup   alfalfa sprouts
½ cup   other sprouts
1   avocado, chopped
6–10   spinach leaves, torn
½   red bell pepper, cut in strips or
     chopped
¼ cup   (or less) broccoli florets, tips only,
     broken very small
Optional: 1–2 tomatoes, cut in thin wedges
     or chopped

Be sure to choose very fresh sprouts for the best flavour and digestibility. To make them more digestible and to avoid their carcinogenic properties, rinse them very thoroughly to remove *all* the brown hulls. Toss gently with other ingredients and serve with your favourite dressing.
Makes 2–4 servings.

Beet Treat

E · G · S · Y · B · Gr

1–3   beets, grated
     juice of 1–2 fresh lemons
     lettuce leaves, spinach leaves *or*
     avocado halves

Mix the beets and juice together and serve on lettuce or spinach leaves, or in or around an avocado half. Delicious!
The lemon juice in this salad makes the beets taste sweet, and the salad is a good treat for your liver. Makes 2 servings.

Beet Treat Salad E · G · S · Y · B · Gr

1 avocado, chopped
6–8 large lettuce leaves (leaf, red,
romaine, bibb *or* Boston), torn
1 green bell pepper, sliced in rings
¼–½ cup sprouts (lentil, mung, alfalfa *or*
other), hulls removed
2–4 beets, grated

Toss together all ingredients except the beets. Dish out the salad and spread beets over the top.

Serve this salad with lemon juice or Lemon Herb Dressing (page 59) for the best flavour. Makes 2–4 servings.

Carrot Confetti Salad

E · G · S · Y · B · Gr

4–6 small or medium carrots, grated
6–10 radishes, sliced paper thin
1 red bell pepper, cut in strips, then
chopped
½ small zucchini, grated
¼–½ cucumber *or* English cucumber,
quartered, then sliced thin

Grate carrots extra fine for digestibility, if desired. Combine all ingredients and toss together in an oil-based or creamy dressing. Make sure to chew this salad well.

Makes 2–4 servings.

Avocado Boats E · G · S · Y · B · Gr

1 large avocado, cut in half, unpeeled

1 Tbs. almonds *or* filberts (hazelnuts)
1 Tbs. cashew pieces *or* pecans

1 Tbs. sunflower seeds
Optional: ½–1 Tbs. raisins or currants
Optional: 2 tsp. shredded unsweetened coconut

Scoop out 1–2 Tbs. of avocado from each half, and store it for use in another recipe. Mix the remaining ingredients together and fill up each avocado half. Place the avocado halves on a bed of lettuce or spinach leaves, topped with yogurt (if tolerated), yogurt substitute, some sesame tahini thinned with nut milk or an oil-based dressing. Serve extra nuts on the side, if desired.

This delightful little salad makes a refreshing change from traditional green, leafy salads. Chew it well. Makes 2 servings.

Wild Zucchini Rice Salad
E · G · S · Y · B

½ cup dry wild rice and brown rice, mixed
1–2 small zucchini, grated
1 tomato, cut in wedges or chunks
1 red, yellow *or* purple bell pepper,
      cut in strips
½ (or less) bunch spinach, torn small
1 avocado, cut in chunks

Cook the rice (½ dry rice makes about 1 cup cooked), cool and chill thoroughly. Combine all the ingredients and toss in your favourite dressing.

This makes a great meal for two, or a prelude to a meal for four. Makes 2–4 servings.

Millet or Quinoa Salad   E · G · S · Y · B

Choose any leafy green salad as a base for this recipe. Add ½–1 cup cooked millet or quinoa and ½ cup or more nuts or seeds, if desired. Toss all ingredients in an oil-based or creamy dressing, and enjoy! Nuts are best if chopped or soaked in water ½–1 hour before using.

DRESSINGS · DIPS · SPREADS

Herb and Oil Dressing
E · G · Y · B · Gr · can be S

1 ¼ cups	light, cold-pressed oil
2–4 Tbs.	apple cider vinegar
2 tsp.	dried parsley flakes, crushed
1 tsp.	*each* sea salt, paprika, tamari soy sauce (wheat-free)*
½ tsp.	basil
¼ tsp.	*each* sea kelp, marjoram, thyme
several dashes	cayenne pepper
Optional:	½–1 tsp. vegetable broth powder *or* onion powder

Mix, beat or blend the ingredients together well and refrigerate for about 2 hours so the flavours can mingle. Beat the dressing or shake well occasionally during chilling time. Serve chilled or at room temperature with salads.

You may blend in 1–2 green onions *or* 1–2 cloves garlic for added flavour.

*Instead of the tamari, you may use ¼ tsp. extra sea salt.

Lemon Herb Dressing
E · G · S · Y · B · Gr

Follow the directions for Herb and Oil Dressing, above, but omit the vinegar and tamari. Add 2–4 Tbs. freshly squeezed lemon juice and increase the sea salt to 1 ¼ tsp. if desired. Blend in 2 green onions or 1–2 cloves garlic for added flavour, to taste.

Cucumber Dill Dressing
E · G · S · Y · B · Gr

1	large cucumber, peeled, seeded and chopped
1–2 tsp.	dill weed
½ cup	light, cold-pressed oil and/or water (there is some loss of flavour with water)
several dashes	cayenne pepper and sea kelp sea salt to taste
Optional:	1–2 cloves garlic, crushed

Blend all ingredients well, chill and serve. Best used within 5 days.

This is a great dressing for low-fat diets, when water is substituted for some of the oil.

Avocado Dressing
E · G · S · Y · B · Gr

2	medium avocados
3–4 tsp.	chopped fresh parsley
½ cup	green onion tops only, chopped
½ cup	light, cold-pressed oil *or* ¼ cup water and ¼ cup lemon juice
⅛ – ¼ tsp.	sea salt
few dashes	sea kelp
	cayenne pepper to taste

Blend all ingredients well and serve. Best used within 3 days.

Tomato Dressing E · G · S · Y · B · Gr

1 cup tomatoes, peeled, seeded and
  chopped, *or* 1 cup tomato juice
½ cup light, cold-pressed oil
1-2 green onions
1 Tbs. apple cider vinegar *or* 1-2 Tbs.
  lemon juice
1-2 tsp. honey *or* other liquid sweetener
1 tsp. sea salt, or to taste
½ tsp. *each* paprika and dried parsley
⅛ tsp. *each* basil and oregano
several dashes *each* cayenne pepper and sea kelp

Blend all ingredients until smooth and chill before serving. Keeps 7 or more days in the refrigerator.

Garlic French Dressing
E · G · S · Y · B · Gr

1 cup light, cold-pressed oil
⅓ cup ketchup
¼ - ⅓ cup apple cider vinegar
1-2 cloves garlic, crushed
1 Tbs. honey *or* other liquid sweetener
1 tsp. sea salt
1 tsp. paprika
several dashes cayenne pepper

Blend or beat together all ingredients. Chill and serve. Keeps 7 or more days in the refrigerator.

Thousand Island Dressing
E · G · Y · B · Gr

6 oz. tofu, crumbled
¼ cup nut milk (or more, for desired
consistency)
2–3 Tbs. ketchup
2–3 Tbs. apple cider vinegar
1–2 tsp. tamari soy sauce (wheat-free)
1–2 tsp. finely minced onion
cayenne pepper and sea salt, to taste
Optional: liquid sweetener, to taste

3–4 Tbs. finely chopped pickles *or* pickle
relish

Combine all ingredients except pickles in a blender or food
processor. Stir in the pickles last. Chill and serve. Keeps up to
about 7 days in the refrigerator.

Creamy Onion Dressing
E · G · Y · B · Gr

6 oz. tofu, crumbled
⅓–½ cup nut milk *or* soy milk (or more, for
desired consistency)
3–6 green onions, finely chopped
2 tsp. tamari soy sauce (wheat-free)
1–2 tsp. dried parsley
½ tsp. basil
½ tsp. paprika
sea salt or vegetable sea salt, to
taste
several dashes cayenne pepper
Optional: liquid sweetener, to taste

Combine all ingredients in a blender or food processor, but

reserve some of the chopped green onions. Stir them in after blending, and add liquid sweetener to taste. Chill before serving. Keeps 4–7 days in the refrigerator.

Tahini Tofu Dressing or Dip
E · G · Y · B · Gr

6 oz.	tofu, crumbled
½ cup	sesame tahini
½ cup	light, cold-pressed oil
½–⅔ cup	freshly squeezed lemon juice
¼ cup	water
2 Tbs.	chopped fresh parsley *or* 1 Tbs. dried parsley
2–4 tsp.	tamari soy sauce (wheat-free) *or* 1–3 tsp. dark miso
4–6	green onion tops, chopped
2–3	cloves garlic, minced
½ tsp.	paprika
½ tsp.	sea salt
⅛ tsp.	sea kelp
	cayenne pepper, to taste

Combine all ingredients in blender or food processor, but reserve 2–3 of the chopped green onion tops. Chop them small and stir them in after blending, to add texture. Chill and serve. Keeps 3–5 days in the refrigerator.

*For a vegetable or cracker dip for parties, decrease the oil to ¼ cup and increase the water to ½ cup.

Mild Curry Dressing or Dip
E · G · Y · B · Gr

7–8 oz.	tofu
1 cup	nut milk *or* soy milk
2–3 tsp.	honey *or* other liquid sweetener
1–1½ tsp.	curry powder

½ tsp. turmeric
¼ tsp. *each* paprika, cumin, chili powder
⅛ tsp. ginger
        sea salt or vegetable sea salt, to
          taste
        cayenne pepper, to taste

Combine all ingredients in a blender or food processor. Chill 1 hour before serving as a dressing or vegetable dip. Keeps 4–8 days in the refrigerator.

Spinach Tofu Dip   E · G · Y · B · Gr

1 lb. spinach (2 cups firmly packed)
6–8 oz. tofu, crumbled
2–3 tsp. dried parsley
½ tsp. basil
⅛ tsp. *each* marjoram, oregano, thyme,
          paprika
several dashes *each* cayenne pepper and sea kelp
          vegetable sea salt and/or tamari
          soy sauce (wheat-free), to taste

Steam the spinach 8–12 minutes until tender. Wash the tofu and dry off excess water. Liquefy all ingredients in a food processor, or use a blender, adding a few drops of water if necessary, and stopping occasionally to stir the dip. Correct seasonings according to your own taste. Keeps 3–6 days in the refrigerator.

Serve the dip in hollowed-out vegetables and dip crackers or fresh vegetables in it, or spread it on bread.

Creamy Tofu Spread   E · G · Y · B · Gr

8 oz. tofu, crumbled
⅓ cup sesame tahini
4–5 tsp. tamari soy sauce (wheat-free) *or*
          dark miso

2 Tbs. finely minced onion
1 clove garlic, finely minced or
crushed
1 scant tsp. apple cider vinegar
¼ tsp. sea kelp

Optional ingredients:
½ cup finely chopped green onion tops,
chives *or* nuts
1 tsp. caraway seeds, dill weed *or* cumin
seeds
½ cup finely chopped celery *or* green
pepper

Combine all the ingredients in a food processor or homogenizing juicer, except the optional ingredients, which should be stirred in last.

Use this tasty, high-protein spread to stuff tomatoes, green peppers or celery. It also makes a great spread for sandwiches or crackers. Keeps 3–7 days in the refrigerator, depending on how many fresh vegetables are included.

Tofu Mock Egg Salad   E · G · Y · B · Gr

12–14 oz. tofu, crumbled
2 stalks celery *or* ½ green pepper,
very finely chopped
1 small tomato, seeded, very finely
chopped and towel-dried
1 bunch green onions, tops only,
finely chopped
½ tsp. garlic powder
¼ tsp. paprika
several dashes *each* cayenne pepper and sea kelp
vegetable sea salt, to taste
Optional: several dashes turmeric, for a
yellow colour

Optional: ¼ tsp. celery seed
Optional: 1–2 tsp. crushed dried parsley

Combine all ingredients, mix well and refrigerate. Keeps 2–4 days in the refrigerator.

Serve with crackers or in pita breads or flatbreads. It can also be stuffed in tomatoes, bell peppers or celery.

Gourmet Sunflower Seed Paté (Prize-Winning Recipe)

E · B · can be G

Dry ingredients:

1 cup	sunflower seeds, ground
½ cup	cornmeal, kamut flour *or* amaranth flour
½ cup	nutritional yeast*
2 tsp.	dried parsley flakes
1 ¼ tsp.	basil
1 tsp.	thyme
¾ –1 tsp.	sea salt
½ tsp.	sage
¼ tsp.	sea kelp (important for flavour)

1 ¼ cups	water
2–4	cloves garlic, chopped
1 cup	chopped white or yellow onion (about 1 medium)
2–3 Tbs.	tamari soy sauce (wheat-free)

1 cup	finely grated white potato, unpeeled (about 1 medium) (rinse after grating to remove excess starch)
⅓ cup	light, cold-pressed oil

Mix the dry ingredients together in a bowl. In a blender,

combine the water, garlic, onion and tamari until liquefied. Add the liquid ingredients to the dry and combine. Then stir in the potato and oil and mix well.

Preheat the oven to 350°F. Lightly oil a 9″ glass pie plate and scoop in the paté mixture. Bake about 45 minutes, until set and browned. Let cool 1–2 hours, then chill thoroughly before serving. It may be reheated later if desired. If served cool, allow the chill to be taken off the paté for the best flavour. This paté freezes well.

*Yeast is necessary in this recipe, so those with candida should avoid the paté.

This nutritious appetizer or protein side dish is wonderful served with crackers and breads or vegetable sticks. Makes 6–8 servings.

Veggie Butter   E · G · Y · B · Gr

½ lb.	lecithin spread (sold in health food stores)
½	small green pepper *or* ½ stalk celery, finely chopped
5 Tbs.	tomato paste
1–2 Tbs.	white or yellow onion, minced
1 Tbs.	dried parsley flakes
1 tsp.	*each* garlic powder, oregano and dill weed
½ tsp.	basil
Optional:	sea salt or vegetable sea salt, to taste

Combine all ingredients in a food processor and chill before using. Keeps refrigerated for 1–3 weeks.

A healthy change from butter and very tasty, this is great on breads and vegetables and with many main dishes.

Basic White Sauce

E · G · S · Y · B
(Note: codes differ if variations are used)

1 cup thick nut milk
1 Tbs. arrowroot powder
1 Tbs. white rice flour *or* brown rice
flour*
2 tsp. light, cold-pressed oil
several dashes cayenne pepper and sea salt, to taste
Optional: 1–2 tsp. sweetening

Beat all ingredients together, including any additions, with a wire whisk. Stir the mixture over medium-high heat until it thickens to the desired consistency. Remove from the heat at once to prevent further thickening. Serve hot.

*Instead of the rice flour, you may use kamut flour if gluten is allowed in the diet. Quinoa flour or millet flour may also be substituted, though the sauce will be less white.

Try the suggested variations and create your own new ones. Serve the sauce fresh and hot over steamed or baked vegetables, or vegetable-grain dishes. Delicious, because you make it just the way *you* like it. The basic sauce keeps 2–4 days refrigerated.

White Sauce Variations

1. Add 1–2 tsp. dried parsley *or* 1–2 Tbs. fresh chopped parsley or cilantro.
2. Add ½–1 tsp. dill weed.
3. Add extra cayenne pepper and several dashes ground cumin and coriander.
4. Add ½ cup sautéed sliced mushrooms *or* sautéed chopped onions.
5. Add ¼–⅓ cup chopped chives or green onion tops.
6. Add ¼–½ tsp. paprika.
7. Add 1 beaten egg.

8. Add ¼–½ cup cashew or blanched almond butter or nut pieces.
9. Blend all ingredients with 4 oz. tofu before heating. Add extra spices to taste.
10. Add 2 Tbs. white wine.
11. Blend or mash ½–1 avocado thoroughly and mix it in *after* the sauce is heated. This makes a tasty, lovely green sauce, good hot or cold. If desired, sprinkle on a bit of chopped fresh parsley for extra eye appeal.
12. Add 2 Tbs. sesame tahini.

Create your own variations. There are unlimited possibilities! Most variations keep 2–4 days refrigerated.

Arrowroot Sauce

E · G · S · Y · B · Gr
(check bouillon cubes for S and Y)

2 Tbs. arrowroot powder
1½ cups cool water
2–3 Tbs. tamari soy sauce (wheat-free)
2 vegetable bouillon cubes *or* 2 tsp. vegetable broth powder
several dashes *each* cayenne pepper and sea kelp

Mix the arrowroot thoroughly with the water in a saucepan, using a wire whisk. Add the remaining ingredients and mix well. Cook over medium heat, stirring constantly, until thickened. Keep warm over low heat. Serve over hot vegetables, whole grains or stir-frys. Keeps up to 7 days in the refrigerator, or may be frozen.

Tahini Sauce   E · G · Y · B · Gr

1 small onion, finely chopped
2–3 Tbs. light, cold-pressed oil

1 cup water
1 cup sesame tahini *or* almond, cashew,
    peanut or sunflower butter
2–3 Tbs. tamari soy sauce (wheat-free)
3 tsp. finely grated fresh ginger
1 Tbs. maple syrup *or* other liquid
    sweetener
1 tsp. sea salt
    cayenne pepper, to taste
several dashes nutmeg

Sauté the onion in oil over medium-high heat until tender. Add the remaining ingredients and simmer everything on low heat for about 30 minutes.

Serve hot over steamed vegetables and grains, or hot or cold in recipes like Rice Salad Roll-Ups (page 94).

Mushroom Gravy

E · Y · B · can be G
(check bouillon cubes for Y)

1 ¾ cups water
1 cup mushrooms, sliced thin
⅓ – ½ cup millet flour, quinoa flour *or* kamut
    flour
2–3 Tbs. tamari soy sauce (wheat-free)
1 Tbs. light, cold-pressed oil
1–2 vegetable bouillon cubes
2–3 tsp. vegetable broth powder
    cayenne pepper, to taste
several dashes sea kelp
Optional: sea salt or vegetable sea salt, to
    taste (if unsalted bouillon or
    broth powder are used)

Sauté the mushrooms in the oil. Add the flour and stir constantly over medium-low heat for 1–2 minutes to brown the flour. Add the remaining ingredients and stir with a wire whisk until the sauce is well mixed and there are no lumps. Stir constantly until very hot. Reduce heat to the lowest setting for 10–15 minutes until the sauce is thickened. Stir occasionally while simmering.

Serve over hot vegetables or whole grains and enjoy!

Vegetarian Gravy   E · G · Y · B

2 cups	kidney bean cooking juice*
3 Tbs.	tamari soy sauce (wheat-free)
1 Tbs.	light, cold-pressed oil
3 Tbs.	arrowroot powder
⅓ cup	millet flour or brown rice flour
¼ – ½ tsp.	chili powder, vegetable broth powder or curry powder
¼ tsp.	sea salt
¼ tsp.	sea kelp
several dashes	cayenne pepper

Use previously stored frozen bean juice, or cook ½–1 lb. kidney beans and drain off and save 2 cups of liquid. Use the "muddiest" part of the liquid for this recipe. Use the beans in another recipe, or freeze them for later use.

Combine all the remaining ingredients with the cooled kidney bean juice and stir over medium-low heat until thickened. Correct the seasonings to taste, and serve the gravy on potatoes, rice, whole grains, vegetables and other dishes.

*Instead of the kidney bean juice, you may use pinto or aduki bean juice.

Mock Cheese Sauce with Nutritional Yeast
E · G · S · B

Dry ingredients:
½ cup   nutritional yeast
3 Tbs.   brown rice flour, millet flour *or*
         quinoa flour
4 tsp.   arrowroot powder
½ tsp.   sea salt

1 cup   water
1 Tbs.   light, cold-pressed oil
Optional: 1–2 tsp. Dijon or yellow mustard

Mix the dry ingredients together, then add the water and oil and mix thoroughly with a wire whisk. Stir or whisk over medium heat or a bit higher until the mixture thickens and begins to bubble slightly. Stir in the mustard, heat another 30–60 seconds and serve instead of cheese sauce over vegetables and/or whole grains.

Mock Cheese Sauce with Eggs
G · S · Y · B · Gr

½ cup   light, cold-pressed oil

3   large egg yolks
2 Tbs.   orange juice
¼ tsp.   paprika
⅛ – ¼ tsp.   sea salt
several dashes   cayenne pepper
Optional: dill weed, chives *or* curry powder, to
             taste

Heat the oil until hot but not bubbling. Place all ingredients *except* the oil in a blender and blend at high speed until thickened. With the blender still running, lift the lid carefully and slowly pour in the oil, keeping the blender partially covered with a towel to prevent splattering. Once the oil is added and the mixture has thickened, serve the sauce hot on green vegetables like broccoli, brussels sprouts, kohlrabi, zucchini, cabbage, green beans, asparagus or greens.

It is also great served cold on hot vegetables, or as a dip for raw vegetables.

*You may add extra seasonings or flavourings such as dill weed, chives or curry powder, if desired.

Thanks to Geraldine Trethart for the original recipe.

Tomato Sauce   E · G · Y · B · Gι

2 Tbs.	light, cold-pressed oil
1	large onion, finely chopped
2–4	cloves garlic, minced
1 cup	mushrooms *or* ½ eggplant, finely chopped
4–6	large tomatoes *or* 1 28–oz. (795 mL) can tomatoes, chopped small
12–13 oz.	tomato paste
1–1½ cups	water
2–3	bay leaves
2 Tbs.	tamari soy sauce (wheat-free)*
2–3 tsp.	dried parsley
1 tsp.	*each* basil, oregano and sea salt*
1–2 tsp.	honey *or* other sweetener, to balance flavours
¼–½ tsp.	*each* marjoram, thyme, sea kelp and rosemary*
	cayenne pepper, to taste

Heat the oil in a large cooking pot over medium-high heat.

When the oil is hot, add the onions, garlic and mushrooms and sauté until tender. Then add the tomatoes and cook until they turn to liquid, about 12–20 minutes. Add the tomato paste and water and mix everything together thoroughly. Lastly, add all the herbs and spices and simmer, covered, over very low heat for 40–60 minutes, stirring occasionally. A bit of water may be added for looser consistency. Correct the seasoning to taste and remove the bay leaves before serving or storing. The sauce keeps up to 7 days in the refrigerator, or it may be frozen for later use.

*The tamari and sea kelp are very important to the flavour of this sauce. The recipe may be doubled or tripled, but be sure to use proportionally less sea salt.

This versatile sauce may be served with noodles, vegetables, whole grains, Pizza Breads (page 97), Lasagne (page 98) and Lasagne Rice (page 99).

Lemon Ginger Sauce
E · G · S · Y · B · Gr

½ cup   freshly squeezed lemon juice
4–5 tsp.   honey *or* other liquid sweetener
⅛ tsp.   finely grated ginger *or* ginger
        powder
Optional: ½–2 tsp. arrowroot powder

Mix all the ingredients in a small pan and stir with a spoon, but if arrowroot is used, stir with a wire whisk. (Without arrowroot, the recipe makes a liquid sauce. If you add arrowroot, the sauce is a thick but pourable glaze.) Stir the mixture frequently over medium-high heat until it thickens and clarifies to a golden glaze. Cover the sauce and keep it warm, or serve immediately over hot, cooked green vegetables like broccoli, brussels sprouts, kohlrabi, zucchini, cabbage, green beans, asparagus or greens. It also works as a chilled sauce served over hot vegetables, or for dipping raw vegetables.

The sauce keeps 2–3 days in the refrigerator and can be reheated over low heat.

Pineapple Ginger Sauce
E · Y · B · can be G · S · Gr

8 oz. pineapple juice (fresh or canned)
1 tsp. arrowroot powder
1 tsp. grated ginger root
½–1 tsp. grated lemon rind

2 Tbs. honey *or* other liquid sweetener
1–2 Tbs. freshly squeezed lemon juice,
      strained
few dashes sea salt

Mix the pineapple juice with the arrowroot and heat on medium heat. Stir until thickened, add the ginger and lemon rind and remove from heat. Strain. Add the sweetener, lemon juice and sea salt. Mix and reheat if necessary. Serve over green vegetables. Toasted sesame seeds can be added on top.

Keeps 2–3 days refrigerated and can be reheated or served cold.

Curry Sauce
E · Y · B · can be G · S · Gr

4 Tbs. light, cold-pressed oil
6 Tbs. millet flour, quinoa flour or kamut
      flour, *or* 5 Tbs. potato flour

2 tsp. curry powder
1 tsp. sea salt
3 cups nut milk *or* soy milk
several dashes cayenne pepper, to taste

Heat the oil in a frying pan. When it is hot, add the flour and stir constantly over medium-low heat until it is browned and crumbly. (Potato flour turns orange when cooked. Add it and stir quickly but do not brown it. Add the nut or soy milk soon after adding the flour.) Add the seasonings and milk, and stir over medium heat until it thickens into a sauce.

This sauce makes a simple meal into a feast. Serve it with tofu, whole grains, vegetables or mashed potatoes. Try it with Curried Grains and Vegetables (page 89).

SOUPS

Miso Seaweed Soup

E · G · Y · B · Gr
(check bouillon cubes for G · Y)

1 large onion, chopped
2 carrots, thinly sliced
2–4 stalks celery, chopped
1–2 Tbs. light, cold-pressed oil

6 cups water *or* vegetable stock
1–2 oz. dried seaweed or 4 oz. fresh
(wakame or kombu are best),
rinsed several times and sliced
thin
1–2 vegetable bouillon cubes *or* 1–2
tsp. vegetable broth powder
1–2 tsp. dried parsley
½ tsp. sea salt
several dashes sea kelp
⅓ cup dark miso (brown rice or soy miso
are good) – keep separate

Sauté the onions, carrots and celery in the oil in a pot big enough to hold all the soup. When the vegetables are tender and the onions are slightly transparent, add all remaining ingredients *except* the miso. Let the soup cook, covered, for about 25–35 minutes.

Remove the soup from the heat, take 1 cup of broth from the

soup and stir the miso into it. When the miso is dissolved into the broth, mix it with the rest of the soup and leave covered (away from heat) about 5–10 minutes so the flavours can mingle. Do not cook the miso; this destroys valuable vitamins and enzymes. Serve the soup immediately. Leftover soup can be reheated, but never let it boil.

Keeps refrigerated for 5–6 days. Do not freeze. Makes 4–8 servings.

Mixed Vegetable Soup

E · G · Y · B · Gr
(check bouillon cubes for G · Y)

1–2	potatoes or jerusalem artichokes, unpeeled and cut into small chunks
2	carrots, thinly sliced
1	large onion, finely chopped
1–2 Tbs.	light, cold-pressed oil
6–7 cups	water *or* vegetable stock
1 cup	fresh or frozen peas *or* chopped green beans
2–3	stalks celery *or* 1 green pepper, chopped
1	small zucchini, thinly sliced or chopped
Optional:	1 stalk broccoli, finely chopped
1–2 Tbs.	tamari soy sauce (wheat-free)
3–4 tsp.	vegetable broth powder *or* 3–4 vegetable bouillon cubes
2–3 tsp.	parsley
1½ tsp.	sea salt
½ tsp.	*each* basil, oregano and sea kelp
several dashes	cayenne pepper

Optional: a bit of honey

Optional: dark miso — keep separate

Steam the potatoes and carrots for 10 minutes before making the soup.

Sauté the onions in the oil in a large pot until they are slightly transparent. Then add the water and all the rest of the ingredients, including the steamed vegetables, *but not the miso.*

Cook the soup on low to medium heat for 40–60 minutes until all the vegetables are tender but not soggy and the flavours are developed.

Take 1–2 cups of water with some vegetables from the soup, liquefy it in a blender or food processor, then return it to the soup. This adds flavour and depth and gives the soup a natural thickness. Correct the soup's spices according to personal taste, add a bit of honey to balance the flavours if desired, and add extra water as needed to thin the soup.

After the soup is finished cooking, 1–2 Tbs. miso can be blended with 1 cup of the broth, then added back to the soup for more taste and nutritional value.

Keeps refrigerated for 6–7 days. Do not freeze. Makes 6–8 servings.

Celery and Potato Soup

E · G · Y · B · Gr
(check bouillon cubes for G · Y)

2 cups chopped white potato (about 1 very large), with skin
3 cups celery, chopped
2 cups water *or* light stock

1 large onion, chopped
1 Tbs. light, cold-pressed oil

¼ cup chopped fresh parsley

2 Tbs. tamari soy sauce (wheat-free)
1 vegetable bouillon cube
1 tsp. vegetable broth powder
1 tsp. sea salt
¼ tsp. paprika
          cayenne pepper to taste

2 cups celery, chopped
½ cup water

⅓–½ cup celery leaves, lightly chopped

Rinse the chopped potato thoroughly to remove excess starch. Simmer the potatoes with the 3 cups celery in the 2 cups water or stock, until tender. While these are cooking, sauté the onion in the oil until slightly transparent. Use a blender to blend all the ingredients *except* the remaining 2 cups celery, ½ cup water and celery leaves. In the original simmering pot, simmer the raw celery and water separately until the celery is somewhat tender. Add the blended mixture to the simmered celery pieces, along with the celery leaves. Stir and simmer everything together on low heat until hot enough to enjoy and serve.

A unique and delicious soup! Keeps 3–5 days refrigerated. Do not freeze. Makes 6–8 servings.

Broccoli Soup E · G · Y · B · Gr · can be S

3–4 stalks broccoli, chopped (about 4
          cups)*
1½ cups cashew milk *or* almond milk
2–3 tsp. parsley
½ tsp. basil
¼–½ tsp. sea salt
several dashes cayenne pepper
Optional: 1–3 tsp. tamari soy sauce
          (wheat-free)

Choose high quality broccoli, as it is very important to the flavour of the soup.

Steam the broccoli until tender, then blend with the nut milk and herbs. Put the soup in a saucepan and heat to almost boiling on medium heat. (Do not boil or overheat!) Serve immediately.

This is a wonderful, creamy soup, more flavourful than some soups made with cow's milk, as the dairy milk actually detracts from the flavour of the vegetables.

*Zucchini may be substituted for the broccoli, with added herbs and seasonings.

Keeps 3–5 days refrigerated. Do not freeze. Makes 3–4 servings.

Parsley Soup

    4 cups unpeeled, cubed white potato (cut
              in ½" cubes)
    1 cup   water
    1 bunch spinach leaves

    1½ cups nut milk
    1 cup   lightly chopped fresh parsley
    1–2 Tbs. light, cold-pressed oil
    1 vegetable bouillon cube
    1 tsp. vegetable broth powder
    2–3 Tbs. tamari soy sauce (wheat-free)
    2–3 tsp. chopped white onion
    1 tsp. *each* paprika and basil
              vegetable sea salt, to taste

    1 cup   very finely chopped fresh parsley
              (at least twice as fine and twice
              as much as the previous amount)

Rinse the potato several times to remove excess starch. Simmer the potato in the water for 10 minutes or until tender. After the potatoes have been cooking for 2–3 minutes, add the spinach leaves on top of them and continue simmering, covered, until tender, about 7–10 minutes longer.

Blend the simmered vegetables and any remaining cooking water with all the other ingredients *except* the 1 cup finely chopped parsley. Put the blended soup mixture in a medium saucepan and stir in the finely chopped parsley. Bring the mixture just to a boil and let it simmer on low heat for 10–15 minutes as the flavours mingle. Correct the seasoning as desired. Serve garnished with extra sprigs of fresh parsley or chopped green onion tops.

Parsley is an iron-rich vegetable, so serve this soup often. It keeps fresh for 3–6 days refrigerated. Do not freeze. Makes 4–6 servings.

Carrot Soup   E · G · Y · B · Gr

4 cups	carrots, slivered and steamed until tender
1½–2 cups	vegetable steaming water *or* vegetable stock
1–2 Tbs.	unrefined, cold-pressed oil
2 Tbs.	tamari soy sauce (wheat-free)
2 tsp.	parsley
1 tsp.	dill weed *or* tarragon, crushed
½ tsp.	sea salt
several dashes	sea kelp
	cayenne pepper, to taste
Optional:	1 tsp. fresh onion or garlic, crushed, *or* ¼ tsp. onion or garlic powder, *or* a few crushed mint leaves (dried or fresh)

Liquefy all ingredients in a blender or food processor until smooth. Then heat the soup in a saucepan on low to medium heat, just up to boiling. Do not boil. Serve hot, garnished with chopped chives, green onions or chopped fresh parsley if desired.

Keeps 3–5 days refrigerated. Do not freeze. Makes 4 servings.

Garlic and Greens Soup

E · G · Y · B · Gr

10–12 medium-large cloves garlic, sliced
¼ cup unrefined, cold-pressed oil

4 large cloves garlic, pressed
4 cups water *or* stock
4–5 green onion tops (green part only),
       finely chopped
½–1 bunch spinach, chopped
¼ cup tomato juice
1–2 Tbs. parsley
1 tsp. vegetable sea salt
½ tsp. sea kelp

3–4 Tbs. dark miso

Sauté the garlic slices in the oil on low to medium heat until thoroughly browned. Remove and discard the garlic. Add the water and all the remaining ingredients *except* the miso. Simmer 20–25 minutes. Remove 1 cup of liquid from the soup and stir the miso into it until it is completely dissolved, then return the liquid to the soup and stir.

This robust yet light soup is very healing and strengthening. It is especially good for colds and flu. It is best eaten within 3–5 days. Do not freeze. Makes 4 servings.

Black Bean Soup

E · G · Y · B · Gr

2 cups dry black beans
10 cups water *or* vegetable stock
1–2 Tbs. light, cold-pressed oil
1 large onion, chopped

                2–3 cloves garlic, minced
                  2 medium carrots, finely grated
                  2 stalks celery, finely chopped
              3 Tbs. dried parsley

              3 Tbs. unsulphured Barbados molasses
            2–3 Tbs. tamari soy sauce (wheat-free)
                  3 bouillon cubes
              2 tsp. *each* cumin and coriander
              1 tsp. sea salt
              ½ tsp. ground cloves
    several dashes sea kelp
                    cayenne pepper, to taste
                    alfalfa sprouts, chopped fresh
                      parsley, green onions *or* chives,
                      for garnish

Soak and cook beans, following the directions for How to Cook Beans Properly (page 26). You should have about 5 cups of cooked beans. After cooking, add enough water or stock to the cooked beans to make 10 cups total.

In a large skillet, heat the oil on medium-high heat and sauté the onion, garlic, carrots, celery and parsley until very tender. Then add the sautéed mixture to the beans, along with the remaining ingredients. Cook everything together for 15–20 minutes to blend the flavours. Correct the seasonings as desired, garnish and serve hot. The soup keeps 7–8 days in the refrigerator and freezes well.

Black beans are exceptionally high in many nutrients, including protein, phosphorous, potassium, calcium and iron. Makes 10–12 servings.

Lentil Soup   E · G · Y · B · Gr

              1 cup dry brown or green lentils
              4–6 stalks celery *or* 2–3 stalks broccoli,
                    chopped

<pre>
        2 carrots, sliced
        1 large onion, chopped
      1–2 cloves garlic, minced
  5 cups water or stock

   2 Tbs. light, cold-pressed oil
   2 Tbs. tamari soy sauce (wheat-free)
   3 tsp. dried parsley
   1 tsp. each sea salt and vegetable broth
              powder
   ½ tsp. each basil, oregano and thyme
   ⅛ tsp. cayenne pepper
several dashes sea kelp
  Optional: ½ tsp. dill weed
</pre>

Add the dry lentils and vegetables to the water or stock and bring to a boil on high heat. Reduce the heat and simmer for about 1 hour, or until the lentils are very tender. Add the remaining ingredients and simmer 15–20 minutes longer, stirring occasionally. Serve hot and enjoy. Keeps 7–8 days in the refrigerator, or may be frozen for later use. Makes 5–6 servings.

MAIN DISHES

PREPARING MAIN DISH GRAINS

Make sure to read About Whole Grains (page 24).

Natural buckwheat and pot barley. Use about 2 cups water per 1 cup grain. Bring the grain to a boil, then turn down the heat to a low bubble. Cover and simmer 20–30 minutes or until tender and no longer crunchy, adding extra water if needed. Cook onions with the grain, and add herbs and salt during the last 10 minutes of cooking time.

Kasha (toasted buckwheat). Cook the same as natural buckwheat, but use a bit less water and reduce the cooking time to 15–20 minutes.

Job's tears. Bring 2–3 cups water and 1 cup of the "seed" to a boil. Reduce the heat to a simmer (make sure there are small bubbles forming in the water) and cook for about 60 minutes or longer, until very tender. Serve with a sauce or vegetables as this is quite robust all by itself. It can also be mixed with other whole grains or used in soups, stews or casseroles instead of barley, buckwheat or brown rice. Job's tears is tolerated by some people with gluten allergies, but check with your health specialist before using.

Millet (main dish). Cook the same as rice, but use 2½ cups water per 1 cup dry millet. It usually does not need pre-washing. Simmer 40–55 minutes and use as a substitute for rice in rice dishes. This is one of the best grains, high in vitamins and very alkaline.

Quinoa. Cook the same as the cereal quinoa (page 42) and use in place of rice or millet in rice or millet dishes.

Whole oats and spelt. These must be soaked in 2 ½ cups water per 1 cup oats for several hours or overnight before cooking. Then change the water and simmer for 45–60 minutes. The oats will be slightly chewy but not crunchy when done. Cook until tender for the best digestion. The grains can be cooked separately or with other whole grains.

Whole rye. Soak and cook the same as whole oats or spelt, above, but use it sparingly because it is strong and bitter. Mix it with oats or spelt in a ratio of 1 part rye to 6–10 parts oats or spelt, and cook them together. Rye adds zest to simple meals, but its flavour does not appeal to everyone.

Short- and long-grain brown rice. Put rice in a pot and fill it with water. Rub the rice together with your fingers and swish it around to remove extra starches, dirt and stray husks. Discard all the water. If the water was very cloudy during the first washing, repeat the process once or twice until the water is relatively clear. Put 2–2 ¼ cups water per 1 cup rice in the pot. Bring to a boil over medium heat, then cover, turn down the heat and simmer 45–60 minutes. When the rice is no longer crunchy but easy to chew and tender, not soggy, it is done. Onions, herbs and spices can be added during the last 15–20 minutes of cooking time. Keep the pot tightly covered while cooking, but it won't hurt to peek!

Wild rice. This is one of the few main dish grains that sometimes requires soaking before cooking. Wash and then soak 1 cup rice in 2 cups water for 2–4 hours. Only by experimenting can you find out whether your wild rice needs soaking. Many varieties can just be cooked, but if they are still hard after 1–1½ hours of cooking, turn off the heat, let them cool and cook them again until tender. Next time, pre-soak it! Then cook the rice as you would cook brown rice. Wild rice is very expensive and rich-tasting, so it is often mixed with brown rice for a delicious, light-tasting, less expensive dish. Cook the two rices separately and mix before serving, or cook wild rice for 15–20 minutes, then add the brown rice to it and cook them together for 45–60 minutes longer. Add extra water if needed.

Stir-Fried Vegetables with Whole Grains

1–2 cups	brown rice, quinoa, millet, buckwheat, kasha or other whole dry grain
3 Tbs.	toasted sesame oil *or* other cold-pressed oil
1	large onion, chopped
¼–½ cup	ginger root, peeled and sliced thin

Hard vegetables:

2	carrots, sliced on a long slant about ⅛″ thick
1	green pepper *or* 1 stalk broccoli, chopped in long, thin strips
2–4	stalks celery, sliced on a long slant about ¼″ thick
1–2 cups	chopped bok choy *or* Chinese cabbage, chopped

Extra vegetables and tofu:

2–3	cloves garlic, minced
½–1 cup	mung bean sprouts *or* snow peas (deveined)
Optional:	1 can water chestnuts, sliced

Optional: 4 oz. tofu cutlets *or* plain tofu, cut
in small cubes

2–5 Tbs. tamari soy sauce (wheat-free)
Optional: several dashes *each* cumin powder,
coriander, cayenne pepper
Optional: ½ cup or more black bean sauce *or*
other Oriental sauce *or* bouillon
broth *or* other flavouring

Cook the whole grain until tender (page 86). While it is
cooking, heat an Oriental wok, iron skillet or frying pan with
the oil until hot and sizzling. Add the onion and ginger and
sauté for 2–3 minutes, stirring, until somewhat tender.

Add the hard vegetables and sauté another 3–6 minutes until
fairly tender. Keep the heat just high enough so the vegetables
keep sizzling the entire cooking time. Keep stirring.

Add the extra vegetables and tofu (if using) and sauté another
1–2 minutes. Then add the tamari and any extra flavourings
and stir another minute or two before serving immediately on
a bed of hot whole grain. Makes 2–4 servings.

Curried Grains and Vegetables

E · G · Y · B · can be S

1 cup whole dry grain (rice, millet,
quinoa, kasha or other grain)
1 cup chopped mushrooms *or* onions
1 cup chopped broccoli
1 cup chopped carrots *or* yellow squash
½–1 cup tofu chunks or cutlets, *or* other
protein pieces
1 recipe Curry Sauce (page 75)
avocado slices
Optional: thin tomato wedges *or* small
steamed carrot sticks

Cook the grain. You should have 2–2½ cups when it is cooked. During the last few minutes of cooking time, steam the vegetables. Spread the cooked grain about 1″ thick on a warmed serving platter. Next spread the tofu or protein over the grain in an even layer, then mound the steamed vegetables on top. Top it off with the curry sauce, so that the sauce covers the centre and dribbles down the sides of the "mountain." Decorate the top and sides with avocado slices and tomato and/or carrot sticks if desired. Put any extra sauce in a gravy server, as people usually like extra sauce.

This is a delightfully mild yet flavourful dish, a beautiful work of art for company and festive occasions. Keep the platter in a warm oven until serving. Reheat leftovers easily by simmering in a covered pan with a bit of water. Makes 4 servings.

Whole Grain-Almond Pilaf E · G · B

¾–1 cup whole dry grain (rice, millet,
quinoa, kasha or other grain)
1 Tbs. light, cold-pressed oil, preferably
toasted sesame oil
1 onion, chopped
8–12 mushrooms, sliced thin*
½ cup almonds *or* other nuts, roasted (see
Roasted Nuts, below) and sliced
2 Tbs. dried parsley *or* cilantro
2–3 Tbs. tamari soy sauce (wheat-free)

Cook the grain. You should have 2 cups when it is cooked.

Heat the oil in a frying pan until hot. Add the onions and sauté until nearly tender. Add the mushrooms, almonds and parsley and sauté 2–3 minutes longer until the onions are clear. Mix the sautéed mixture with the hot cooked whole grain and tamari. Serve hot and enjoy.

*Shitake or oyster mushrooms can be used if desired to add a spectacular flavour to this dish.

This is a great main dish or side dish. Makes 2–4 servings.

Roasted Nuts

Use whole, raw nuts that are as fresh as possible. Preheat the oven to 300°F. Spread the nuts in a single layer in a low, dry pan and bake. Whole almonds take about 10 minutes, most other nuts take 2–6 minutes. When cooled, slice thin or chop for use in recipes. These roasted nuts are also very tasty in salads, and they can also be ground and sprinkled on cereals.

Stuffed Green Peppers E · G · S · Y · B

1 cup dry brown rice *or* millet, *or* ¾ cup
dry quinoa

1–2 Tbs. light, cold-pressed oil
1 large onion, very finely chopped
2 very large or 4 smaller carrots,
finely minced or grated
2–3 tsp. dried parsley *or* ⅓ cup chopped
fresh parsley
1 tsp. sea salt
½ tsp. *each* basil, oregano and paprika
⅛ tsp. *each* marjoram, thyme and sea kelp
several dashes cayenne pepper

Optional: ½ cup cooked chick peas

4–6 green or red peppers, cut in half
lengthwise
1–2 Tbs. sesame seeds *or* chopped
sunflower seeds

Cook the brown rice or millet in 2 cups or a bit more water for 50–60 minutes until the grain is tender and fairly dry. (Cook the quinoa for 20–30 minutes in 2½–3 cups water.) In a large skillet, heat the oil and sauté the onions, carrots and herbs until the vegetables are slightly tender. Then add the cooked grain and chick peas to the skillet and sauté for 5 minutes or more so the flavours can mingle.

Preheat the oven to 350°F. Place the raw peppers cut side up in large baking dishes (with sides 2" high or more). Fill the pepper shells with the vegetable-grain mixture. Top the grain-filled peppers with raw or toasted sesame seeds or sunflower seeds. Fill the bottom of the baking dish around the peppers with about ½" or more of water. Bake for 15–25 minutes until the grain is lightly browned and the peppers are tender but still slightly crisp.

Serve hot with Vegetarian Gravy (page 71) or Arrow-root Sauce (page 69) spread over the top. Makes 4–6 servings.

Tofu Stuffed Zucchini   E · G · Y · B

4–6 small zucchini, ends removed, cut in half lengthwise

2 Tbs. light, cold-pressed oil
2–3 green onions, diced
½ cup finely chopped green pepper
7–8 mushrooms, chopped, *or* ⅓ cup diced eggplant, sautéed

14–16 oz. tofu
2–3 tsp. tamari soy sauce (wheat-free)
½ tsp. sea salt
½ tsp. curry powder
several dashes cayenne pepper
Optional: several dashes turmeric, for yellow colour

Steam the zucchini for 4–7 minutes until slightly tender. Remove a sliver of zucchini from the inside of each slice to create a centre cup or groove, if desired. In a frying pan, heat the oil and sauté the onions, pepper and mushrooms for about 2 minutes. Add the tofu and remaining ingredients, *except* zucchini, and sauté for a few minutes more until the flavours mingle. Preheat the oven to 350°F.

Place the strips of zucchini centre side up in a low baking dish with about ¼″ of water on the bottom. Cover the zucchini with the tofu mixture, taking care not to spill any in the water. Bake for 10–15 minutes until everything is hot and tender throughout. Serve immediately as a main dish with a cooked whole grain. Makes 4–6 servings.

Vegetable and Tofu Shish Kebabs

E · G · Y · B

Cut several of the following foods into pieces ¼ – ¾″ x 1–2″ (use about 2 cups per person):

pineapple, in chunks

citrus slices

green, red or yellow bell peppers, in 1–1½″ chunks

zucchini, in ¼″ thick rounds

mushrooms, small whole, or cut in half

potatoes, in 1″ chunks (pre-steamed 10 minutes)

broccoli, in small "trees" (pre-steamed 5 minutes)

cauliflower, in 1½″ chunks (pre-steamed 5 minutes)

tomatoes, in 1½–2″ chunks

Tofu Cutlets (page 96) or tofu from Rice Salad Roll-Ups (page 94), in chunks

onions, in wedges

whole snow peas (edible pea pods)

*Use one or more of the following
sauces:*
Garlic French Dressing (page 61)
Thousand Island Dressing (page 62)
barbecue sauce
Tomato Sauce (pge 73) (Use 3
    parts Tomato Sauce mixed with
    1 part tamari or dark miso)
tamari soy sauce (wheat-free)

Using 2 or more 12″ bamboo or stainless steel skewers per person, select a variety of vegetables and tofu. Place the foods on the spears alternately, to fill each spear completely. Use a cooking brush to baste the kebab with sauce, choosing only one sauce for each kebab, and baste generously. Broil the kebabs for 4–10 minutes (depending on your broiler type) until tender and juicy. Serve immediately over hot cooked brown rice, millet, quinoa, buckwheat, kasha or other whole grain. Pour the juices from the broiler pan over the grain for added flavour.

Rice Salad Roll-Ups with Tofu and Tahini Sauce

Tofu sauté:
½–1 lb. tofu
2 tsp. light, cold-pressed oil
2–4 Tbs. tamari soy sauce (wheat-free)
several dashes cayenne pepper

1 pkg. large, round rice wrappers

Filling ingredients:
1–2 cups mung bean sprouts, washed
1 cup or more mung noodles *or* Chinese
        noodles *or* brown rice, cooked
1–2 red peppers, cut in thin strips

3–9 lettuce *or* spinach leaves, cut in
strips or shredded
Optional: 1 bunch green onions, whole,
cleaned and trimmed
Optional: 2 carrots, grated

1 recipe Tahini Sauce (page 69), hot or cold

Cut the tofu in strips the size of ¼" wide french fries. Heat the oil in a small skillet and add the tofu strips. Sauté 1 minute and add the tamari and cayenne. Sauté 1 minute longer and set aside to cool, or keep warm.

Take 2 rice wrappers and dip them together in warm (not hot) water for 30 seconds or until softened. Lay them on a clean, flat surface. Start placing the filling ingredients on the lower middle of the wrappers. Lay them in a horizontal line, about 2" above the bottom of each wrapper. For each roll-up, use 1 Tbs. of the sprouts, 1 Tbs. of the noodles (or rice), several strips of pepper, a few strips of lettuce and a bit of carrot.

Fold in the right and left sides of the wrapper and tuck the white bulb of a green onion under *one* of the folds, letting the green top stick out over the other folded side. Then, from the bottom, roll the wrapper as tightly as possible without tearing it. It rolls up just like a burrito.

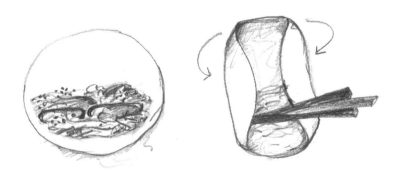

Serve the Tahini Sauce for dipping before each bite. Two or three roll-ups makes a complete lunch or light supper. Makes 4–6 servings.

Tofu Cutlets   E · G · Y · B · Gr

2–3 lbs. pressed tofu, or regular tofu if
      pressed is not available

4 cups water or vegetable stock
⅔ cup tamari soy sauce (wheat-free)
2 Tbs. chili powder*
1 Tbs. onion powder*
1 Tbs. garlic powder*
½ tsp. sea kelp
several dashes cayenne pepper

Freeze the tofu solid, then defrost in warm water until thawed. Freezing texturizes the tofu and helps separate out some of the water. Rinse and gently hand press as much water as possible from the tofu. Slice it into ¼" thick slices and cut these into pieces 1½–2" long. Press them dry with paper towels.

Combine all of the remaining ingredients in a pot twice the size of the ingredients, and bring it to a boil, stirring occasionally. When it boils, lower the heat and let it simmer, covered, for 12–15 minutes. Add the tofu pieces and simmer everything together for 30 minutes longer so that flavours can be absorbed into tofu pieces. Stir the liquid occasionally and turn the tofu pieces. Remove the tofu from the liquid and serve hot or cold as a snack or side dish, or add it to recipes. Makes 2–3 lbs.

The tofu cutlets can be chilled and eaten on the run as occasional nutritious "meal replacements." They can also be eaten as cold hors d'oeuvres with toothpicks, sliced for sandwiches, or served on crackers as canapes. They can be used instead of meat in many recipes. Crumble them in tomato sauce or lasagne. Use pieces of tofu cutlet in stir-fried vegetables, tempura, shish kebabs, casseroles, rice dishes or in many other main dishes. You can broil them for a few minutes on each side, which gives them a unique, succulent flavour that even surpasses their deliciousness when served hot or cold as described above. Enjoy this wholesome treat often! And serve it with a whole grain whenever possible.

Store any leftover plain tofu in glass containers for 1–2 weeks in the refrigerator, or freeze individual servings in plastic freezer bags for up to 3 months.

*Chili powder may be omitted if one of the variations (recipes follow) is prepared. Onion and garlic powder may be omitted with little loss of flavour in any of the three variations.

Curried Tofu Cutlets

Follow the directions for Tofu Cutlets, above, but omit the chili powder and add 2–3 tsp. curry powder and ½ tsp. turmeric. *Optional:* add ¼ tsp. *each* cumin and coriander.

Green Herb Tofu Cutlets

Follow the directions for Tofu Cutlets, above, but omit the chili powder and add 1 Tbs. dried parsley flakes, 1 tsp. basil, ¼ tsp. oregano and ¼ tsp. marjoram. Crush the herbs with a mortar and pestle or by hand just before adding them to the recipe.

Pizza Breads   E · can be G · Y · B

1–3 slices bread per person
            Tomato Sauce (page 73)
            Tofurella® *or* other tofu cheese,
              grated

            Toppings:
            pineapple chunks, tomato slices,
              zucchini slices, green or red
              pepper strips, sliced olives,
              sliced mushrooms

Heat the tomato sauce while heating the broiler. Toast any type of bread and spread on the hot tomato sauce. Sprinkle on tofu cheese and an assortment of toppings. Place the breads on aluminum foil or a flat baking tray and broil for 1–4 minutes, until the cheese is melted and everything is hot and bubbly. Keeps 1–2 days in the refrigerator.

Pizza Breads make a good snack or a whole meal. Refrigerate the leftovers — they make a great cold lunch the next day.

Lasagne   Y · B · can be E · G

8–12 oz.	corn, rice, quinoa or spelt noodles, lasagne or fettuccine style
4–5 cups	Tomato Sauce (page 73)
8 oz.	tofu cutlets *or* plain tofu, crumbled
1–1½ lb.	tofu cheese, mozzarella style, grated
½ lb.	tofu cheese, cheddar or Monterey jack style, grated

Preheat the oven to 350°F. Undercook the noodles so they are still a little bit chewy, or *al dente*. Rinse them under cool water and drain before using.

Lightly oil a 9x13″ baking pan. Spread 1¼ cups of the Tomato Sauce evenly on the bottom of the pan. Add a layer of half the cooked noodles. Mix the 2 grated cheeses together and cover the noodles with half the cheese mixture.

Next, spread on half the remaining sauce and then all of the crumbled tofu. Top everything off with the remaining noodles and the rest of the sauce. Bake for 20–25 minutes, then remove the pan from the oven and evenly spread on the remaining cheese. Bake again immediately for 15–20 minutes longer, until everything is hot and bubbly. Remove from the oven and let it set about 10 minutes before serving. Makes 6–8 servings.

Note: Some tofu cheeses contain a protein-dairy derivative called casein.

Lasagne Rice   E · G · Y · B

Follow the directions for Lasagne, above, but instead of the noodles use 6 cups or more cooked brown rice (about 3 cups dry). Another whole grain like quinoa, millet or buckwheat may also be substituted for the noodles.

Spaghetti Squash Pasta

A golden coloured winter squash with orange pulp, called spaghetti squash, is available in vegetable markets nearly all year round. It gets its name from its delightful stringy, spaghetti-like texture and flavour, and it can be used to make grain-free, pasta-like spaghetti.

Boil the squash whole for 1 hour or more until tender, or cut it in half lengthwise and bake it for 45–60 minutes. Then scoop out the pulp and serve it with your favourite sauce (see page 68).

NOODLES

See the Buying Guide (page 177), for addresses of noodle suppliers, and visit local stores to check for availability elsewhere. These ready-to-cook noodles are available:

Buckwheat noodles (Westbrae). Cook in about 8 minutes.

Corn noodles (Deboles). Various cooking times, depending on style of noodles. Check packages for directions.

Mung noodles (Canasoy and Chinese stores). Cook in about 12 minutes.

Quinoa noodles (Quinoa Corp.). See package for cooking times, corn is also added. Other varieties without corn are available in some areas.

Rice noodles (Canasoy, Eden and Chinese stores). Cook in about 8–10 minutes.

Brown rice noodles (Pastariso). Cook in 8–11 minutes.

Wild rice noodles (Northern Lights). Package says to cook 2–4 minutes but I suggest 8–14 minutes.

Soy-rice noodles (Canasoy). Cook in 12–15 minutes.

Spelt noodles (Del Bonita and Purity Foods). Cook in 10–12 minutes.

Preparing Noodles

Bring a large pot of water to a boil. When it is bubbling hard, add the noodles. Most noodles expand to 2–3 times their size. Mung noodles expand to 6–8 times their size.

After adding the noodles, wait for the water to boil again, then turn down the heat *but make sure the water keeps bubbling*. Be careful not to overcook, as some of these noodles will fall apart or get very mushy from overcooking.

Cook until tender and serve with your favourite sauce (see page 68).

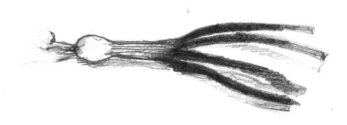

BEAN MAIN DISHES

See How to Cook Beans Properly for Good Digestion (And No Gas!) (page 26).

Sweet and Sour Lentils

E · G · S · B · Gr

1 cup brown lentils
2 ¼ cups water or vegetable stock
1 small or ½ medium onion, chopped
3–4 Tbs. apple cider vinegar
3–4 Tbs. honey*
1 Tbs. light, cold-pressed oil
1 tsp. basil
½–¾ tsp. sea salt

Cook the lentils in the water or stock for 30 minutes. Add the onions, cover and cook 20–25 minutes longer. After 50–55 minutes total cooking time, if most of the water is not cooked out or absorbed by the lentils, uncover the pan and cook 10–15 minutes longer or until most of the liquid is gone and the lentils are fully cooked tender. Stir gently as needed, 2–3 times.

Add all the remaining ingredients and cook 5–8 minutes longer, until the flavours of the spices mingle with the lentils. The lentils will be like a *very thick* soup or stew. Add extra seasonings if desired, and serve with rice, millet or other whole grain dish and vegetables.

*Instead of honey, you may use 2–3 Tbs. maple syrup, but it is not recommended, as it alters the flavour somewhat.

Makes 3–4 servings.

Middle Eastern Falafels

E · G · B · Gr

1 cup dry chick peas
½ cup sesame tahini
1 clove garlic, minced

1–2 tsp.　grated or very finely chopped onion
2–4 tsp.　tamari soy sauce (wheat-free)
2 tsp.　dried parsley
1 tsp.　cumin seeds or powder (cominos)
1 tsp.　chili powder
½–1 tsp.　sea salt
¼ tsp.　celery seed
¼ tsp.　sea kelp
several dashes　cayenne pepper, to taste

Soak the chick peas and cook until very tender, then drain them and save the liquid. While the chick peas are still very hot, mash them together with the remaining ingredients. Add ½–1 cup of the reserved cooking liquid as needed to make a spreading consistency. Herbs and spices may be adjusted to taste.

Use the falafel as a sandwich spread with one or two of the following: avocado, sprouts, lettuce, spinach and tofu cheese. Toast the sandwiches in a toaster oven for an extra special treat. This recipe makes about 6 hearty sandwiches. The spread is also wonderful on crackers or stuffed in fresh celery sticks, for hors d'oeuvres or snacks. A few tablespoons, hot, makes a good main dish as well—the spread is tastiest when hot. You may use a bit less liquid in the spread and add a bit of flour, roll the falafel into balls and pan-fry them, or shape them into patties and pan-grill them. Traditionally, falafel balls were deep-fried, but this is an unnecessary addition of fats to the diet.

Leftover spread can be refrigerated for up to 6 days, or stored in the freezer. Save the cooking liquid and add as needed to soften the spread.

Incredible Chili
(Prize-Winning Recipe)　　　E · G · B · Gr

2½ cups or 1 lb. dry kidney beans*

2–3 Tbs.　light, cold-pressed oil
2 cups　chopped onion

4 cloves garlic, minced
Optional: 1–2 green peppers, chopped fine
4 medium tomatoes, chopped small
12–13 oz. tomato paste
2 Tbs. tamari soy sauce (wheat-free)*
3 tsp. chili powder
1–1½ tsp. sea salt
1 tsp. oregano
1 tsp. dried parsley
½ tsp. sea kelp
¼ tsp. cumin seeds or powder (cominos)
⅛ tsp. cayenne pepper, or to taste
Optional: 1 tsp. crushed red chili peppers

Soak the beans overnight or 6–8 hours in 7–8 cups water. Drain off any leftover soaking water and rinse the beans well. Cook the beans in enough water to cover them plus 1″. Bring the beans to a boil on high heat and scoop off any foam that rises to the surface as they boil. Reduce the heat so that the water is still slightly bubbling and simmer, covered, 1¼–1 ½ hours until the beans are *very* tender and not chewy. (See How to Cook Beans Properly, page 26.)

While the beans are cooking, heat the oil in a large skillet and sauté the onions and garlic for 2–3 minutes. Add the green peppers, wait a minute or two, then add the tomatoes and simmer 10 minutes. Add all of the remaining ingredients *except* the beans, and simmer on low heat for 45–60 minutes to develop the flavour.

When the beans are ready, drain them and save the liquid. Mix the sauce and beans together and add some of the reserved liquid if needed to bring the chili to the desired consistency. Cook the chili on low heat for 15–20 minutes or more so the flavour of the sauce mingles with the beans. Serve hot, or cool the chili and refrigerate it for reheating the next day.

Note: The amount of cayenne determines the "hotness" of the chili. If only mild cayenne is available, use 1–2 tsp. or to taste.

*Tamari soy sauce may be omitted, with a slight change of flavour. Pinto or aduki beans can be substituted for the kidney beans, with some loss of flavour and texture.

Keeps 7–8 days in the refrigerator, or may be frozen.

Leftover bean liquid may be refrigerated or frozen and used in other recipes, like Vegetarian Gravy (page 71). A large batch of sauce can be made in advance and frozen in a few individual containers, to be used in a hurry for quick meals. Beans can be made fresh each time for more vitamins and flavour, but they can also be frozen with the sauce. Makes 8 servings.

Pinto Bean Tacos   E · G · B

2 cups dry pinto beans*
1–2 onions, chopped
2–3 Tbs. tamari soy sauce (wheat-free)*
3 tsp. chili powder
1 tsp. sea salt
⅛ tsp. or less cayenne pepper
several dashes sea kelp
Optional: (to balance flavours) 1–2 tsp.
honey *or* maple syrup

12 corn tortillas

2–3 cups chopped vegetables for topping:
any combination of chopped
lettuce, spinach, sprouts, onions
or chives, tomatoes, green
pepper, cucumber, avocado,
mushrooms
Optional: Tomato Sauce (page 73), chili
sauce *or* salsa
Optional: guacamole

To prepare the pinto beans, follow the directions for cooking kidney beans in Incredible Chili (above), or see How to Cook

Beans Properly (page 26). During the last 15 minutes of cooking time, add the onions and cook until tender. Drain and save the cooking liquid from the beans. While the beans are still hot, mix in all the herbs, spices and sweetener if desired.

Mash most of the beans with a masher, fork or food processor. Use a little of the reserved cooking liquid to bring the beans to a thick but very spreadable consistency. Leave some beans whole in the mixture, for varied texture.

Take the tortillas from the refrigerator or directly from the freezer and put them in the oven (once frozen and defrosted, they tend to curl up). Toast them in a 400°F oven for 60 seconds or longer, until lightly toasted and somewhat stiff but still flexible. Add the hot bean mixture, selected toppings and/or sauces, and serve.

To reheat leftover taco beans, see Refried Beans (recipe follows). Or, spread a ¼" thick layer of cold taco mixture on toasted tortillas and place them under a heated broiler for 4–10 minutes until hot and crispy. Cover with toppings and serve.

*Tamari soy sauce may be omitted, with a slight change of flavour. Kidney or aduki beans may also be substituted for the pinto beans.

Tacos can be a complete meal all by themselves. This recipe serves 6–8. Leftover bean cooking liquid may be refrigerated or frozen for other recipes like Vegetarian Gravy (page 71).

Chili Tacos   E · G · B

Follow the directions for Pinto Bean Tacos, above, but instead of taco beans or tomato sauce, use warm chili. Be sure to use chili of a firm, not runny, consistency. Leftover rice or millet can be added to the chili to thicken it.

Refried Beans   E · G · B · Gr

Heat taco beans in a lightly oiled frying pan for 10–15 minutes, or until warmed. Stir frequently over low to medium heat. Serve with salsa and guacamole or corn chips.

BREADS

Please read Kitchen and Baking Tips (page 17), and Important Tips on Baking Breads (page 18).

Rice Bread ✓   G · S · Y

CRUMBLY

Wet ingredients:
- 2 large eggs, beaten
- 1 cup milk substitute*
- 2 Tbs. light, cold-pressed oil
- 2–3 Tbs. honey *or* 1½–2 Tbs. maple syrup*

Dry ingredients:
- 2½ cups brown rice flour
- ¼ cup tapioca flour or amaranth flour or buckwheat flour (*or* brown rice flour or rice polish)
- 1 tsp. cream of tartar*
- ½–1 tsp. baking soda*
- ½ tsp. sea salt
- ¼ tsp. allspice *or* cinnamon

Preheat the oven to 350°F. Beat the eggs well, add the rest of the wet ingredients and mix well. Sift the dry ingredients together in a separate bowl, then slowly add them to the wet, beating briskly with a wire whisk. Pour or scoop the batter into a lightly oiled and floured bread pan and smooth the top of the batter so it is evenly spread. Bake 45–50 minutes. Large cracks may appear on top of the loaf, but this is natural for gluten-free breads.

When the bread is nicely browned, remove it from oven and cool 10–15 minutes before slicing. This bread is crumbly only around the edges, but it holds together well, is firm and has a delightful, light flavour.

*Instead of 1 cup milk substitute and sweetener, 1 1/8 cups fruit juice may be used. Pear, peach and apple are good, and you may experiment with other naturally sweet juices. If only water can be used as a liquid, use 7/8 cup and make sure to include the 3–4 Tbs. of liquid sweetener. In place of the cream of tartar *and* soda, you may use 2½–3 tsp. baking powder. 1 tsp. guar gum may be added for a less crumbly bread texture.

Rice Bread Variation   G · S · Y

Follow the directions for Rice Bread, above, but omit ½ cup brown rice flour and use ½ cup cooked, cold brown rice or sweet brown rice. Bake the bread at 375–400°F for 45–50 minutes.

Millet Bread   G · S · Y

Wet ingredients:
2 large eggs
1 cup milk substitute*
2 Tbs. light, cold-pressed oil
2–3 Tbs. honey *or* 1½–2 Tbs. maple syrup

Dry ingredients:
2 cups millet flour
½ cup tapioca flour
¼ cup arrowroot flour
1 tsp. cream of tartar*
½ tsp. baking soda*
½ tsp. sea salt
½ tsp. allspice *or* cinnamon

Follow the directions for Rice Bread, above.

*It is best *not* to use water in place of milk substitute in this recipe.

Millet Bread Variation   G · S · Y

Follow the directions for Millet Bread, above, but omit ½ cup millet flour and use ½ cup cooked, cold millet. Bake the bread at 375–400°F for 45–50 minutes.

Buckwheat-Millet Bread   E · G · Y

Wet ingredients:
¼ cup light, cold-pressed oil
¼ cup honey *or* maple syrup *or* fruit
          concentrate
2·cups nut milk*
2 Tbs. liquid lecithin

Dry ingredients:
1 cup millet flour
1 cup buckwheat flour
½ cup brown rice flour
2 Tbs. arrowroot powder
4 tsp. baking powder (wheat-free)
1 tsp. sea salt
¼ tsp. cinnamon

Preheat the oven to 350°F. Combine the oil and liquid sweetening and mix thoroughly. Add the rest of the wet ingredients. Sift dry ingredients together in a separate bowl, then slowly add them to the wet ingredients, beating briskly with a wire whisk. Pour the batter into a lightly oiled large loaf pan, and bake 50–60 minutes, until a toothpick comes out clean. Wait at least 10–15 minutes before gently removing the bread from the pan.

This bread is a bit crumbly, so cut it carefully.

*If your diet allows for eggs, you may substitute 2 large beaten eggs for ½ cup of nut milk, *or* add 2 tsp. of guar gum for a stronger bread.

This is a delicious, wholesome, hearty brown bread, good for everyday use. It refrigerates well or may be frozen.

Cranberry Surprise Bread   E · G · S · Y

1 cup whole cranberries

Wet ingredients.
1 ¼ cups Sweet Cranberry Sauce (page 156)
¾ cup honey*
¼ cup light, cold-pressed oil
2 tsp. vanilla extract

Dry ingredients:
1 ½ cups millet flour
½ cup brown rice flour *or* tapioca flour
4 tsp. baking powder (wheat-free)
4 tsp. arrowroot powder
1 tsp. cinnamon
¼ tsp. sea salt

¼ – ½ cup nut milk *or* soy milk
½ cup chopped walnuts *or* pecans

Wash and simmer the whole cranberries with 2–3 Tbs. water on low heat until tender but not mushy, about 5–9 minutes. The cranberries should hold their shape. Set aside.

Preheat the oven to 350°F. Combine the wet ingredients and mix well. Sift the dry ingredients together in a separate bowl, then add the dry ingredients to the wet and combine well. Add just enough of the nut milk to make a thick but pourable batter. Fold in nuts and cooked cranberries.

Scoop the batter into an oiled and floured loaf pan and bake 55–65 minutes, until the top is nicely browned and a toothpick comes out clean. Let the bread cool before removing from pan and slicing.

*Instead of honey, you may use ½ cup maple syrup and ¼ cup juice or water. ¼ cup of the flour may be omitted and ¼ cup powdered sweetening added for a sweeter, nicer-textured bread if desired. 1–2 tsp. guar gum may also be added as a binder.

Oatmeal Bread   E · Y

Wet ingredients:
1½ cups nut milk *or* soy milk
½ cup honey*
2 Tbs. light, cold-pressed oil
2 Tbs. liquid lecithin

Dry ingredients:
1 cup oat flour
¾ cup brown rice flour
¼ cup soy flour *or* oat flour
4 tsp. baking powder (wheat-free)
1 Tbs. arrowroot powder
1 tsp. sea salt
¼ tsp. cinnamon
1 cup rolled oats

Preheat the oven to 375–400°F. Combine the wet ingredients. In a separate bowl, sift together all dry ingredients except rolled oats, then stir in the oats. Add the dry ingredients to the wet and mix well. The batter will be stiff but stirrable.

Scoop the batter into a lightly oiled loaf pan and smooth into place. Bake 1–1¼ hours, until loaf is firm and lightly browned, and a toothpick comes out clean. If the top gets too dark before the loaf tests done, cover loosely with a tent of aluminum foil for 10–15 minutes, and remove foil for the last 10 minutes of baking time. Cool thoroughly before removing from pan and slicing.

*Instead of honey, you may use 6 Tbs. maple syrup and 2 Tbs. extra nut milk or soy milk. Add 1 tsp. guar gum for stronger bread.

Oatmeal-Raisin Sweet Bread   E · Y

Wet ingredients:
1 cup   honey *or* other liquid sweetener
1 cup   nut milk *or* other milk substitute
1 cup   raisins *or* currants
2 Tbs. light, cold-pressed oil
2 Tbs. liquid lecithin

Dry ingredients:
1 cup   oat flour
¾ cup   brown rice flour
¼ cup   soy flour *or* oat flour
4 tsp. baking powder (wheat-free)
4 tsp. arrowroot powder
1 tsp. cinnamon
½–1 tsp. sea salt
1 cup   rolled oats

Follow the directions for Oatmeal Bread, above. Lightly oil and flour the loaf pan before baking.

Millet-Rice Bread   E · G · Y

Wet ingredients:
1 ¼ cups   milk substitute
½ cup   honey *or* other liquid sweetener
2 Tbs. light, cold-pressed oil
2 Tbs. liquid lecithin

Dry ingredients:
2 cups   millet flour
¾ cup   brown rice flour

4 tsp. baking powder (wheat-free)
1 Tbs. arrowroot powder
1 tsp. sea salt
¼ tsp. cinnamon

Follow the directions for Oatmeal Bread, above. Use a bit more milk substitute if necessary.

Zucchini-Carrot Bread or Muffins with Kamut (Energy Bread)   E · S · Y

½ cup cooked quinoa, millet *or* other grain

Wet ingredients:
½ cup finely grated zucchini, towel-dried
½ cup finely grated carrot, well-packed
½ cup crushed pineapple, drained
¾ cup honey, maple syrup *or* fruit
        concentrate
¼ cup light, cold-pressed oil
½ cup apple, pear *or* peach juice
1–2 tsp. vanilla extract

Dry ingredients:
2 cups kamut flour*
3–4 tsp. baking powder (wheat-free)
¼ tsp. sea salt

Optional: ½ cup raisins *or* chopped nuts

To cook the quinoa, simmer 3 Tbs. dry quinoa in 6 Tbs. of water for 20 minutes. Mix all the wet ingredients together thoroughly and gently. Stir in the cooked quinoa. In a separate bowl, sift together the flour, baking powder and sea salt.

Preheat the oven to 350°F. Lightly oil a large loaf pan. Line the bottom with waxed paper and oil the waxed paper. Lightly flour the pan and shake out excess. Combine the wet and dry ingredients thoroughly until a slightly stiff but stirrable batter forms. Fold in raisins or nuts. Scoop batter immediately into pan and spread smooth. Bake 55–60 minutes until bread is lightly browned and a toothpick comes out clean. Cool 15 minutes or more before removing from pan and slicing.

For muffins, bake at 375–400°F for 20–40 minutes.

*Instead of kamut flour, you may use oat flour *if* 2 tsp. guar gum is also added.

Cornbread or Corn Muffins
G · S · Y · can be E

Wet ingredients:
1 cup   milk substitute
2–3 Tbs.   honey
2 Tbs.   light, cold-pressed oil
1   egg, beaten, *or* egg substitute*

Dry ingredients:
2 cups   medium or fine cornmeal*
1 Tbs.   baking powder (wheat-free)
½ tsp.   sea salt

Preheat the oven to 400°F. Combine wet ingredients thoroughly. Sift dry ingredients together in a separate bowl, then add to wet ingredients and beat well.

Oil a loaf pan or 18 muffin cups and pour in the batter. Bake the loaf 25–35 minutes, until loaf is golden and a toothpick comes out fairly clean. Bake the muffins 15–25 minutes.

*If the cornmeal is too coarse, substitute ½ cup *pure* corn flour for ½ cup of the cornmeal. Instead of the egg, you may use 1/3 cup extra water, 1 Tbs. arrowroot powder and 2 tsp. guar gum.

Corn Tortilla Breads

Preheat the oven to 350–400°F and lightly toast purchased corn tortillas on oven racks for 1–2 minutes. Use them instead of regular breads with meals, beans or for sandwiches. They can also be wrapped around rice, whole grains, beans and/or vegetables and baked 10–20 minutes at 350°F.

Flatbreads   E · G · S · Y · B · can be Gr

½ cup buckwheat flour, millet flour *or*
          amaranth flour
½ cup brown rice flour *or* tapioca flour
2 tsp. arrowroot powder

2 tsp. light, cold-pressed oil
½ cup water

⅓–⅔ cup extra flour, for kneading

Sift the flours with the arrowroot powder. In a separate bowl, mix the oil and water, then add to the flour mixture. Work the dough with a fork and then your hands. Knead briefly and roll into a ball. Divide the ball into 8 parts. Roll each part into a ball and pat flat. Sprinkle each bread with flour and roll between 2 sheets of waxed paper with a rolling pin. Turn frequently while rolling, and lift the waxed paper occasionally to add flour so the dough does not stick. The bread should be somewhat rounded and about ⅛″ thick.

Preheat the oven to 400°F. Lightly oil a frying pan and heat to medium-high. Put one flatbread in the pan and heat 15–20 seconds on each side. Immediately put bread in oven and heat 3 minutes. Turn over and heat 1½–2 more minutes. The bread will puff up a bit in the oven, but not as much as traditional pita because it has no yeast. Re-oil the pan with a paper towel dipped in oil, and repeat procedure for each flatbread.

Cool breads before storing in plastic bags, or eat them hot from the oven.

A gluten-free, pita-like bread. Makes 8 breads.

Chick Pea Chipatis   E · G · S · Y · Gr

1 cup chick pea flour
⅓ cup water
2 Tbs. arrowroot powder
1 Tbs. light, cold-pressed oil
Optional: ¼ tsp. sea salt

Mix all ingredients well. Roll into 1″ balls and pat flat. With a rolling pin, roll out pastry-like rounds.

Heat a lightly oiled frying pan until very hot. Reduce heat to medium-high and heat each round for 1–2 minutes on each side, until warmed and slightly browned. Serve hot or store in the refrigerator.

Chipatis may be eaten hot from the pan, or cold, or lightly toasted. They are wonderful with rice or Indian foods, and they make a good bread substitute for sandwiches. This recipe makes 8–10 chipatis.

Flatbreads to Buy

Lentil papadams (labelled as "biscuits"). These flat, brown lentil flour breads are made with chilis, salt and various spices. They taste and crunch like potato chips, go well with Indian and other foods, and are great for snacking. To prepare, preheat the oven to 350°F and place them on oven racks until they begin to bubble and curl. They will become crispy *after* being removed from the oven. Or, drop them one by one into a pan of boiling oil for about 1 minute, until they curl up and bubble a bit. Remove from oil, drain and eat hot or cold.

Rice wrappers (labelled as "rice paper"). Look for thin, round rice paper breads 8–12″ in diameter. Dip them in warm (not hot) water and wrap cooked rice, noodles, fish, chicken, tofu and/or vegetables in them. Eat them as is, heat in the oven and cover with your favourite sauce, or make Rice Salad Roll-Ups (page 94).

Yeasted Rice Bread   G · S · B

4 tsp.   baking yeast
½ cup   very warm (not hot) water, about
             112–118°F

1 Tbs.   maple syrup *or* 2 Tbs. honey

1 cup   pear juice, apple juice *or* peach
             juice*
2   eggs, beaten foamy

Foam stage flours:
½ cup   tapioca flour
½ cup   white rice flour*
¼ cup   arrowroot powder
2 cups   brown rice flour

1 tsp.   sea salt
2 Tbs.   light, cold-pressed oil

3 cups   brown rice flour
2 tsp.   light, cold-pressed oil
¼ cup   extra flour, for kneading

Stir the yeast into the very warm water for 1–2 minutes with a wire whisk. Let it sit for 3–5 minutes. Stir in the maple syrup and set aside for 5 more minutes.

Meanwhile, heat the juice to 110–118°F (so it will keep the batter warm). Add the warm juice and beaten eggs to the yeast mixture. Mix well, then add the foam stage flours in the order given, ½ cup at a time, mixing well after each addition. After the 2 cups brown rice flour is added, place the bowl of batter in a warm (not hot!) place (above or beside a warm stove is good). Let it rise 35–45 minutes until doubled in size.

Gently stir in the sea salt and the 2 Tbs. oil. Slowly add the 3 cups brown rice flour, ½ cup at a time until the mixture thickens, then ¼ cup or a few tablespoons at a time. Mix the dough with your fingers when it is too stiff to mix with a spoon.

When all 3 cups of brown rice flour are added and the dough is solid but not heavy, rub a large bowl with the 2 tsp. oil and place the dough in it. Turn the dough over once or twice to cover all sides with oil. Cover the bowl with 2–3 layers of damp paper towels. Let it rise 1–1½ hours. Then punch it down and let it rise again for 1–1½ hours. This really helps to develop the dough.

Lightly oil 1 large or 2 smaller bread pans, and coat lightly with tapioca flour (for mildness). Punch down the dough in the bowl and divide it in two if desired. Knead the loaf (loaves) with the extra ¼ cup flour. Shape into 1 or 2 loaves and place in the pan(s). Let rise 40–45 minutes until nearly doubled in size. (Don't let it rise longer than 45 minutes, or the bread may fall during baking.)

Preheat the oven to 350°F. With about ¼ tsp. of oil, lightly oil the top of the loaf (loaves) to keep cracks from forming on top. Bake 50–60 minutes for 1 large loaf and 40–50 minutes for 2 smaller loaves, or just until very firm and slightly browned around the edges. It is natural for *small* cracks to cover the top of the bread.

*Instead of fruit juice, you may use a milk substitute if these directions are followed:

1. Double the maple syrup or honey.
2. Add ¼ cup extra tapioca flour.
3. Add ½ tsp. cinnamon or allspice to the recipe.
4. Omit juice and add 1 cup warm milk substitute.

If white rice flour is not available, use ¼ cup extra tapioca flour and ¼ cup extra arrowroot powder.

This bread is delicious all by itself, and it also makes great French toast. This recipe makes 1 large loaf or 2 small loaves.

Yeasted Millet Bread   G · S · B

Follow the directions for Yeasted Rice Bread, above, but use fine millet flour instead of brown rice flour. Omit the ½ cup white rice flour and add ¼ cup extra tapioca flour and ¼ cup extra arrowroot powder. If juice is used, add ½ tsp. cinnamon. If milk substitute is used, add 1 tsp. cinnamon, double the sweetener (as above) and add ¼ cup extra tapioca flour.

Yeasted Rye Bread   S · B

Follow the directions for Yeasted Rice Bread or Yeasted Millet Bread, above, but use 2 cups fine rye flour in place of the first 2 cups brown rice flour or millet flour. Add 1 Tbs. caraway seeds if desired.

CAKES

Apple-Millet Bread or Tea Cake

Wet ingredients:
1 cup Applesauce (page 155)
¾ cup honey*
½ cup apple juice (or a bit more, if the
    applesauce is more solid)
¼ cup light, cold-pressed oil
2 tsp. vanilla extract
3 Tbs. liquid lecithin

Dry ingredients:
2 cups millet flour
½ cup brown rice flour *or* millet flour
½ cup tapioca flour
2 Tbs. arrowroot powder
4 tsp. baking powder (wheat-free)
1 tsp. sea salt
½ tsp. cinnamon

Apple layer:
1-2 large Spartan *or* MacIntosh apples,
    chopped small and steamed until
    tender
1 tsp. cinnamon

Preheat the oven to 350°F. Combine the wet ingredients well.

Sift the dry ingredients together in a separate bowl. Lightly oil a 9x9″ cake pan or 2 loaf pans. Add the dry ingredients to the wet ingredients and mix thoroughly. Spread half the batter evenly into the pan. Spread half the steamed apple evenly over the batter and sprinkle with ½ tsp. cinnamon. Carefully and evenly spread on the remaining batter, being careful not to press down on the apples. Sprinkle with the remaining ½ tsp. cinnamon, then spread on the remaining apples in a thin, even layer.

Bake 40–50 minutes, until a toothpick comes out fairly clean. Wait at least 10–15 minutes before gently removing from pan.

*Instead of honey, you may use ½ cup maple syrup and ¼ cup extra apple juice, or ¾ cup fruit concentrate. For a sweeter "cake," omit ¼ cup of the apple juice and add ¼ cup extra liquid sweetening. You may also add 1 tsp. guar gum for a stronger bread.

Banana Bread or Cake E · G · Y

Follow the directions for Apple-Millet Bread, above, but omit the steamed apple. Instead of 1 cup applesauce, add 1 cup mashed banana. In place of the apple juice, use nut milk. 1–1½ cups chopped walnuts or pecans may be stirred into the batter just before baking. Spread half the batter into the baking pan, sprinkle with ½ tsp. cinnamon, spread on the remaining batter, and sprinkle with the remaining ½ tsp. cinnamon. Extra nuts may be added on top. For a sweeter "cake," omit ¼ cup of the nut milk and add ¼ cup extra liquid sweetening.

Easy Holiday Fruitcake S · B · can be E

1 cup raisins *or* currants
1 cup chopped dates
1 cup chopped prunes *or* figs
1 cup chopped dried apricots
1 cup chopped dried pears *or* pineapple
1–1½ cups chopped pecans *or* fresh walnuts

1 cup   apple cider *or* apple juice, at room
           temperature
¾ cup   maple syrup *or* other liquid
           sweetener
½ cup   light, cold-pressed oil
     3   extra large eggs *or* 4 medium eggs
           or equivalent egg substitute
1 tsp.   sea salt
1–2 tsp. grated lemon rind

½ cup   very warm apple cider *or* juice
           (about 110–115°F)
2 Tbs. baking yeast

2½ cups kamut flour*

1 cup   amaranth flour or buckwheat flour
           (for darker cake), *or* 1 cup
           millet flour, brown rice flour or
           oat flour (for lighter cake)
Optional: (but adds lots of flavour) 1–2 tsp.
           rum flavouring or extract

Combine the chopped dried fruits and nuts with the apple cider
or juice. Mix well, then let the mixture stand so the fruits can
absorb most of the liquid.

In a separate bowl, mix the liquid sweetening with the oil,
then add eggs (if any) and beat well until a bit foamy. Add the
sea salt, lemon rind and liquid part of egg replacer (if any) and
mix again.

In a smaller bowl, combine the warmed apple cider or juice
and baking yeast with a wire whisk. Set aside for 10 minutes.

Add the dried fruit mixture to the egg mixture along with all
the flour and dry egg replacer (if any). Mix well. A very stiff
but stirrable dough will form. Then add the yeast mixture and
rum, and mix everything thoroughly to make a loose batter.

Place batter in a bowl twice its size, cover with a damp towel and let rise in a warm place for 1½-2 hours.

Stir well and spread in an oiled, waxed-papered and floured 9x13″ pan. Let rise ½ hour, not longer or it may fall when baked. If it rises too long, stir it down and let it rise again for 20–25 minutes before baking.

Preheat the oven to 350°F. Bake cake 45–55 minutes until nicely browned.

*Instead of kamut flour, you may use oat flour *if* 2 tsp. guar gum is also added.

Even people who think they don't like fruitcake love this delicious cross between cake and bread. Serve it at holiday time, or any time.

Carob Cake   G · S · Y · can be E

Wet ingredients:

1½ cups	honey*
¾–1¼ cups	nut milk
½ cup	light, cold-pressed oil
4	eggs, beaten*
2 tsp.	vanilla extract
Optional:	1 Tbs. orange or lemon rind, finely grated

Dry ingredients:

1½ cups	brown rice flour *or* millet flour
¾ cup	tapioca flour*
¼ cup	arrowroot powder
⅔ cup	carob powder, dark roasted
4 tsp.	baking powder
½ tsp.	sea salt
Optional:	1–2 tsp. guar gum

¼–½ cup	chopped pecans, walnuts, filberts *or* pine nuts

Optional: shredded unsweetened coconut to
taste

Preheat the oven to 325°F. Combine the wet ingredients, using just ¾ cup of the nut milk to start, and mix well. In a separate bowl, sift together the dry ingredients, then add slowly to the wet ingredients, beating with a wire whisk or a mixer. The mixture should be thick, but pourable. If it is too dry, gradually add the remaining nut milk as needed.

Beat the batter 100–200 strokes until smooth, then mix in the nuts. Lightly oil a 9x13" cake pan or 3 - 8" or 9" round cake pans, and dust lightly with tapioca flour. Pour in the cake batter and bake 50–65 minutes until the cake is lightly browned and a toothpick comes out clean. Cool the cake before removing from the pans and top with Carob Fudge Topping (page 155). Sprinkle coconut on top if desired. Keep refrigerated, or slices may be frozen.

*Instead of tapioca, you may use buckwheat flour. Instead of honey, you may use 1¼ cup maple syrup and ¼ cup extra nut milk. Instead of eggs, you may use powdered egg substitute and the required liquid replacement.

"Wild" Spice Cake   G · S · Y

1½ cups honey*
½ cup brown date sugar *or* barley malt
powder *or* natural raw sugar

Wet ingredients:
1 cup nut milk
⅔ cup light, cold-pressed oil
2 eggs, beaten*
2 tsp. vanilla extract

Dry ingredients:
2 cups millet flour*
¾ cup brown rice flour *or* tapioca flour*

¼ cup soy flour, amaranth flour,
            buckwheat flour *or* other flour*
4 tsp. baking powder (wheat-free)
3 tsp. arrowroot powder
2 tsp. cinnamon
1½ tsp. nutmeg
¾ tsp. ground cloves
½ tsp. sea salt

½–1 cup nut milk

Preheat the oven to 350°F. Lightly oil and flour a 9x13" cake pan or 3 - 9" round cake pans.

Mix the honey and date sugar together in a large bowl. Add the wet ingredients and mix well. In a separate bowl, sift together the dry ingredients. Gradually add the dry ingredients to the wet and beat together, adding as much of the remaining ½–1 cup nut milk as necessary to make a slightly thick, but pourable batter. Bake 1 hour or until the cake is lightly browned and a toothpick comes out clean.

This cake is delicious with Date Fluff Frosting (recipe follows). Frosted slices may be kept refrigerated or frozen.

*You may use 3 cups of millet flour instead of the combination of flours. Instead of honey, you may use 1¼ cup maple syrup and ¼ cup extra nut milk. Instead of eggs, powdered egg substitute and the required liquid replacement may be used.

Date Fluff Frosting   G · S · Y · B · Gr

⅓–⅔ cup nut milk
½ lb. pitted dates
¼ cup honey
3 Tbs. arrowroot powder
3 tsp. real vanilla flavouring

4 egg whites, beaten stiff

Blend ⅓ cup of the nut milk with all the other ingredients, *except* the egg whites. If the mixture is too thick, gradually add the remaining nut milk. Fold the date mixture gently into the beaten egg whites with a spoon or wire whisk. Chill the frosting 1–2 hours, then spread it on a cool cake and chill the whole cake before serving. Keep refrigerated, or slices may be frozen.

Perfect Pumpkin Cake   G · S · Y

Wet ingredients:

2–2½ cups honey*
2 cups cooked, mashed pumpkin (see
      Pumpkin for Recipes, below)
¾ cup light, cold-pressed oil
4 eggs, beaten*
2 tsp. almond extract
2 tsp. vanilla extract

Dry ingredients:

2½ cups millet flour *or* rice flour
½ cup buckwheat flour, soy flour *or*
      amaranth flour
4 tsp. cinnamon
4 tsp. baking powder (wheat-free)
3 tsp. arrowroot powder
1 tsp. sea salt

Optional ingredients:

1 cup chopped walnuts *or* pecans
1 cup raisins *or* currants

Preheat the oven to 350°F. Lightly oil and flour a 9x13″ cake pan or 3 - 9″ round cake pans.

Mix the wet ingredients together. In a separate bowl, sift the dry ingredients together. Gradually add the dry ingredients to the wet and mix well. The batter should be slightly thick, but pourable. Fold in the optional ingredients. Bake 1 hour or until the cake is lightly browned and a toothpick comes out clean.

This cake is delicious with Pumpkin Fluff Frosting (recipe follows).

*Instead of honey, you may use 1½–2 cups maple syrup or fruit concentrate and ½–1 cup apple juice or water, totalling 2½ cups. Instead of eggs, powdered egg substitute and the required liquid replacement may be used.

Pumpkin Fluff Frosting

G · S · Y · B · Gr

    1 cup cooked, mashed pumpkin (see
              Pumpkin for Recipes, below)
    3 Tbs. arrowroot powder
 ½–⅔ cup honey *or* maple syrup
    2 tsp. real vanilla flavouring
    1 tsp. cinnamon
    ⅛ tsp. ginger
    ⅛ tsp. nutmeg
dash sea salt

    4 large egg whites, beaten stiff

Blend all the ingredients, *except* the egg whites, until smooth. Gently mix the pumpkin mixture into the egg whites with a spoon or wire whisk. Chill the frosting 1–2 hours, then spread it on a cool cake and keep the whole cake chilled until serving.

Pumpkin for Recipes

There are several ways to prepare cooked, mashed pumpkin for recipes. Boil a small pumpkin whole, then seed and peel it, drain off the excess liquid and mash it. Cut a large pumpkin into large pieces, seed it, bake at 375–400°F for 45–70 minutes until tender, then peel and mash it. Canned pumpkin may also be used, though it is not as fresh, nutritious or flavourful.

*Some kinds of orange winter squash, such as butternut and buttercup squash, may be substituted for pumpkin.

Fudgy Carob Brownies E · G · S · Y · Gr

Wet ingredients:
¾ cup honey*
¼ cup water
⅓ cup light, cold-pressed oil
2 tsp. vanilla extract

Dry ingredients:
1 cup amaranth flour
½ cup carob powder
⅓ cup arrowroot powder
2 tsp. cream of tartar*
1 tsp. baking soda*
½ tsp. salt

Optional: ½–1 cup chopped nuts or seeds, *or*
1 cup crispy brown rice cereal

Combine the wet ingredients and beat well. In a separate bowl, sift the dry ingredients together. Slowly beat the dry ingredients into the wet and fold in the nuts.

Preheat the oven to 350°F. Lightly oil a 8x8″ or 9x9″ square baking pan, and dust with tapioca flour or arrowroot flour. Scoop in the batter and bake 25–30 minutes. Do not overbake – the brownies should be moist and tender. Cool the brownies before removing them from the pan, and spread with Carob Fudge Topping (page 155) if desired. Store in the refrigerator.

*Instead of honey, you may use ½ cup maple syrup and increase the water to ½ cup. Instead of cream of tartar *and* baking soda, you may use 1–2 tsp. wheat-free baking powder.

Amaranth flour and tapioca flour combine to make this a grain-free dessert with a grain-like texture.

For crisper, sweeter brownies, substitute ⅛–¼ cup powdered sweetener like date sugar, raw sugar or maple sugar for the same amount of amaranth flour.

PUDDINGS · PIES · CANDIES · CRISPS

EASY FRUIT-TOFU PARFAITS

Kiwi-Tofu Parfaits E · Y · B · can be G

2	large kiwi fruits, peeled and sliced
1 lb.	soft tofu *or* regular tofu, crumbled, if soft is unavailable
⅔–¾ cup	honey *or* maple syrup *or* fruit concentrate
2 Tbs.	arrowroot powder
1 tsp.	real vanilla flavouring
Optional:	1–2 tsp. guar gum*

2–4	kiwi fruits, peeled and sliced ⅛" thick
	granola or other crunchy-nut cereal

Mix the 2 large kiwi fruits, tofu, honey, arrowroot, vanilla and guar gum in a blender or food processor. Put 1" or more of the mixture in a parfait glass. Next, place 2 layers sliced kiwi fruit and/or a ½–1" layer of granola or cereal. Then add another 1" or so of the kiwi-tofu mixture, and continue rotating the layers until the glasses are topped with kiwi-tofu mixture. Top off each parfait with a sprinkle of cereal and a ¼" round of kiwi stuck vertically halfway into the topping.

Chill thoroughly in the refrigerator before serving, and

enjoy as a light but nourishing dessert. The parfait keeps 2–4 days in the refrigerator. Makes 4–6 servings.

*The guar gum makes a firmer fruit parfait, similar to one using gelatin. Without it, the parfait is softer and more puddling-like.

Strawberry-Tofu Parfaits

Follow the directions for Kiwi-Tofu Parfaits, above, but replace the 2 kiwis with 1½ cups strawberries. Replace the remaining kiwis with 1–2 cups sliced strawberries for layering.

Blueberry-Tofu Parfaits

Follow the directions for Kiwi-Tofu Parfaits, above, but replace the 2 kiwis with 1½ cups blueberries. Replace the remaining kiwis with 1–2 cups whole blueberries for layering.

Pineapple-Coconut-Tofu Parfaits

Follow the directions for Kiwi-Tofu Parfaits, above, but replace the 2 kiwis with 1½ cups crushed or blended pineapple. Replace the remaining kiwis with 1–2 cups crushed or chunk pineapple for layering. Shredded unsweetened coconut can also be layered and sprinkled on top.

Other Fruit-Tofu Parfaits

Follow the directions for Kiwi-Tofu Parfaits, above, but replace the kiwi fruits with your favourite fresh fruit in season. Try peaches, mangoes, bananas, raspberries – or invent your own parfait.

Jello Parfait   E · S · Y · B · can be G

Use the Agar Agar Jello (recipe follows) instead of the fruit-tofu mixture in the recipe for Easy Fruit-Tofu Parfaits (above).

Agar Agar Jello   E · G · S · Y · B · Gr

¼ oz. (about 6–7 Tbs.) agar agar flakes
    or 2–2½ Tbs. agar agar powder
1 cup cool water
1–1½ qts. fruit juice (apple, grape,
    strawberry, cherry, pear, peach,
    papaya, etc.)*
Optional: cut fruits

Mix the agar flakes in the water and heat up to a boil, stirring as it heats. Once it boils, turn down the heat and simmer until most of the agar is dissolved and it thickens. Stir regularly. Make sure the fruit juice is at room temperature. Pour the juice in a glass or metal bowl and *strain* the agar mixture into it. Stir it and mix everything well. Chill thoroughly until it hardens and gels. When the jello is partially set, about 30–40 minutes or more, add cut fruits to it if desired. Jello is usually ready to eat in 1½–3 hours. Some juice may settle to the bottom of the bowl when the jello is spooned out—this is natural for agar jello.

Note: Most citrus juices do not "set well" with agar. Avoid them, or use just a little mixed with other juices.

Agar is a great gelatin substitute. This jello also makes a nice topping for ice cream.

Carob Mint Tofu Pudding
    E · G · Y · B · Gr

1 lb. soft tofu *or* regular tofu, if soft is
    unavailable
1–1½ cups maple syrup, honey *or* fruit
    concentrate
½–⅔ cup carob powder
2 Tbs. arrowroot powder
3 tsp. real vanilla flavouring
¼ tsp. peppermint extract, or more to taste

several dashes sea salt
Optional: shredded unsweetened coconut

Combine all ingredients in a food processor or homogenizing juicer. (This pudding is too thick for a blender.) Spoon into individual pudding cups and chill thoroughly before serving. A rich dessert. Makes 4 servings.

Almond Carob Tofu Pudding
E · G · Y · B · Gr

1 lb. soft tofu
1–1½ cups maple syrup
⅓–⅔ cup carob powder
¼ cup almond butter
2 Tbs. arrowroot powder
3 tsp. real vanilla flavouring
¼ tsp. almond extract
several dashes sea salt

½ cup slivered almonds
extra slivered almonds, for garnish

Combine all ingredients *except* slivered almonds in a food processor or homogenizing juicer. (This pudding is too thick for a blender.) Stir the ½ cup slivered almonds into the pudding, spoon into individual pudding cups and chill thoroughly before serving. Just before serving, sprinkle a few slivered almonds on top of each serving. The almonds may be toasted if desired. Keeps 5–8 days in the refrigerator. Makes 4 servings.

Rice Pudding
G · S · Y · B

2 cups pre-cooked brown rice, cold
½ cup nut milk or sweet juice (apple, pear or peach are good)

½ cup honey*
2 eggs, beaten
2 tsp. vanilla extract
1–1½ tsp. cinnamon
⅛ tsp. sea salt
Optional: ½ cup raisins, currants, chopped
dates, chopped walnuts *or*
chopped pecans

1 cup of dry brown rice makes about 2 cups of cooked brown rice. Be sure to measure after cooking, however, as rice varieties expand differently. Use sweet brown rice if available.

Preheat the oven to 375°F. Combine all ingredients and mix thoroughly. Spread the mixture in a lightly oiled 9x9″ casserole dish and bake 35–45 minutes, uncovered, until "set" and somewhat firm.

*Instead of honey, you may use 6 Tbs. maple syrup and 2 Tbs. extra liquid.

Serve this delicious, nutritious, easy dessert hot or cold.

Rice Pudding Without Eggs
E · G · S · Y · B

Follow the directions for Rice Pudding, above, but omit the eggs. Add 2–3 Tbs. arrowroot powder and 1 tsp. guar gum or xanthan gum. 1–2 tsp. grated lemon or orange rind may also be added for extra flavour. Add extra liquid sweetener, juice or nut milk if needed.

Pumpkin Pudding G · Y · B · Gr · can be S

2 cups cooked, mashed pumpkin (see
Pumpkin for Recipes, page 126)
1–1¼ cups nut milk
⅓–⅔ cup honey *or* maple syrup
2 large eggs

2 Tbs. arrowroot powder
Optional: 1 Tbs. instant soy milk
powder
2 tsp. vanilla extract
½–1 tsp. cinnamon
¼ tsp. ginger
several dashes *each* nutmeg and sea salt
Optional: 1 Tbs. unsulphured Barbados
molasses

Blend all ingredients and taste the mixture, then adjust the flavourings to taste. The mixture will be somewhat thick, but very pourable.

Preheat the oven to 325°F. Lightly oil 1 or 2 baking dishes and pour the mixture into them to a depth of 1½–2″. Bake the pudding 30–45 minutes until it is firm and turns golden brown. Chill thoroughly before serving.

Serve with Dairy-Free Ice Cream (page 152) or Tofu Whipped Cream (page 158).

Pumpkin Pie G · Y · B · can be S · Gr

Prepare piecrust shells using Nut Crust (page 136) or Crunchy Crust (page 137) recipe. Follow the directions for Pumpkin Pudding (above), pour the pudding into the pie shells and bake as directed. One recipe for Pumpkin Pudding makes 2–3 pies.

You may sprinkle each piece of pie with extra cinnamon and top with Dairy-Free Ice Cream (page 152) or Tofu Whipped Cream (page 158).

Apple Pie E · G · S · Y · B · can be Gr

1 Nut Crust (page 136) or Crunchy
Crust (page 137) piecrust shell

6–8 large baking apples (Rome,
Spartan, MacIntosh, Jonathan,
Newton, Lodi), cored and
chopped (and peeled, if desired)
Optional: ½ cup raisins, currants *or* chopped
nuts

2½ Tbs. arrowroot powder
¼ tsp. sea salt
1½–2 tsp. cinnamon
½–¾ cup honey *or* ⅓–½ cup maple syrup
Optional: 1–2 Tbs. ground nuts

Prepare the piecrust.

Simmer the apples and raisins or currants with ¼ cup water on medium heat for 8–10 minutes, or until tender. Drain the apples and reserve the cooking liquid. When liquid is cool, mix it with the arrowroot powder and sea salt. Add 1–2 Tbs. extra water if needed. Heat it in a saucepan until it thickens, stirring constantly.

Preheat the oven to 375°F. Combine the arrowroot mixture with the apples and all remaining ingredients, and scoop the filling into the piecrust shell. 1–2 Tbs. of ground nuts may be sprinkled on top, for extra flavour and attractiveness.

Bake for 25–40 minutes, until browned and set. (The larger and thicker the pie, the longer the baking time.)

Makes 1 medium or large pie.

Mom's Baked Apples or Apple Crisp
E · S · Y · B · Gr

4 large baking apples (Rome,
Spartan, MacIntosh, Stayman)
chopped walnuts *or* pecans, to taste
Optional: raisins or currants, to taste
½ cup orange juice *or* apple juice
½–¾ cup honey *or* maple syrup

cinnamon for sprinkling
several dashes nutmeg and sea salt

Preheat the oven to 400°F. Core the apples and peel a bit from the tops and bottoms only. Sit them upright in a lightly oiled *glass* or Corningware baking dish. (Orange juice turns green in tin!) Stuff the centres of the apples with chopped nuts and/or raisins or currants. Pour the juice evenly over the apples, then pour liquid sweetener evenly over them. Sprinkle generously with cinnamon and add a dash or two of nutmeg and sea salt on each apple. Bake 30–45 minutes or until the apples are completely tender.

Serve these with any meal or for dessert. They are good hot or cold.

Apple Crisp: Peel the apples completely and chop them into 1–2″ chunks. Place them in a glass or Corningware dish and cover with the remaining ingredients. Sprinkle ½–¾ cup rolled oats, rolled rice or rolled barley on top, for an apple crisp dessert or side dish.

Nut Crust   E · G · S · Y · B · can be Gr

2 Tbs. light, cold-pressed oil
2 Tbs. honey *or* maple syrup *or* fruit
         concentrate
¼ cup arrowroot powder
¼ cup amaranth flour *or* buckwheat flour*
½ tsp. cinnamon
¾ cup ground nuts and/or seeds
         (almonds, walnuts, pecans,
         sunflower seeds)

Preheat the oven to 350°F. Mix the oil and honey, then add the arrowroot powder, flour and cinnamon. Lastly, mix in the ground nuts. Press the crust into the bottom and sides of a lightly oiled small pie pan, but not the upper flat rim of the pan.

For baked pies, bake the crust for 3–5 minutes then allow it to cool for 5–10 minutes. Scoop filling into the crust and bake according to recipe directions. If the top edges of the crust brown too fast while baking, cover the edges with aluminum foil and remove the foil after baking.

For no-bake pies, bake the crust 9–14 minutes or until firm. Cool, scoop in the pie filling and chill. Sprinkle extra ground nuts on top of the filling for a decorative effect and added flavour.

Makes 1 small pie. For a large pie, use 1 ½ times this recipe.

*Instead of amaranth flour, millet or rice flour may be used. This will slightly change the flavour and colour of the crust.

Crunchy Crust   E · S · Y · B

Wet ingredients:
¾ –1 cup honey *or* ⅔ cup maple syrup with
          2–3 Tbs. fruit juice
½ cup light, cold-pressed oil
¾ tsp. sea salt

Dry ingredients:
2½ cups rolled oats, rolled rice *or* rolled
          barley*
1 cup oat flour*
Optional: 2 Tbs. finely grated lemon or
          orange rind *or* finely shredded
          coconut

Combine the wet ingredients and mix well. In a separate bowl, combine the dry ingredients. Slowly add the dry ingredients to the wet and mix well.

Press the crust into a lightly oiled pie pan and add the pie filling. If a top crust is desired, extra crust mixture can be gently pressed into a top crust layer. Bake according to pie filling recipe directions. Use this crust for pies or Date Squares (page 138). For no-bake pies, bake the crust for 4–8 minutes until lightly browned but still slightly tender to the touch. Cool, scoop in pie filling and chill before serving.

*If rolled rice is available, use it with rice flour.

Crispy Date Squares   E · S · Y · B

1 recipe Crunchy Crust (above)
1 recipe Date Spread (page 157)

Preheat the oven to 350–375°F. Press half of the crust mixture into the bottom only of a lightly oiled 9x9″ pan. Next, spread on all of the Date Spread. Lastly, evenly "sprinkle" the remaining crust mixture over the top of the Date Spread, then gently pat it into place as a top crust.

Bake 25–40 minutes, until top is lightly browned but still tender. The crust will harden as it cools, so *do not let the crust harden in the oven, or it will become very* hard when cool. Cut it into squares before it cools completely, or it will be difficult to cut.

A rich dessert or snack. Makes 1 pan, 9x9″.

Tofu Cheesecake   E · Y · B · can be G · Gr

1½ lbs. soft tofu *or* regular tofu
1 cup honey, maple syrup *or* fruit
        concentrate*
¼ cup natural raw sugar (see Food
        Glossary, page 162) *or* barley
        malt powder
3 Tbs. light, cold-pressed oil
3 Tbs. arrowroot powder
2 Tbs. lemon juice
1 Tbs. finely grated lemon rind
1 Tbs. vanilla extract
⅛–¼ tsp. sea salt
Optional: 1 piecrust shell

Mix all ingredients *except* the piecrust in a food processor or homogenizing juicer. Line a 10″ pie plate with the pie crust or, if no crust is used, oil a 9″ pie plate.

Preheat the oven to 350°F. Spread the tofu mixture evenly in the crust or the oiled pie plate, and smooth out the top so the "cheesecake" will be even. Bake for about 45 minutes, or until the cake is set and turns a medium golden colour. Chill thoroughly and serve with Strawberry Topping (page 158) or other fruit topping.

Carob Tofu Cheesecake

E · Y · B · can be G · Gr

22 oz. soft tofu *or* regular tofu
¾ cup liquid sweetener
½ cup roasted carob powder
⅓ cup natural raw sugar *or* barley malt
        powder
3 Tbs. light, cold-pressed oil
3 Tbs. arrowroot powder
2 Tbs. lemon juice
1 Tbs. vanilla extract
⅛ – ¼ tsp. sea salt
Optional: ¼ tsp. peppermint extract
Optional: 1 piecrust shell

Follow the directions for Tofu Cheesecake, above. Serve chilled with Strawberry Topping (page 158) or other fruit topping.

Nutty Carob Balls

E · G · S · Y · B · Gr

½ cup *ground* sunflower seeds, walnuts
        or pecans
½ cup *ground* almonds *or* cashews
½ cup carob powder, dark roasted

½ cup honey *or* ⅓ cup maple syrup and
2½ Tbs. water or juice
1 cup *chopped* almonds, walnuts, pecans
or cashews (chop each nut or
nut half into about 6–10 pieces)
ground nuts, for coating*

Mix the ground nuts and carob powder together. Stir in the sweetener to make a stiff mixture. Work in the chopped nuts, using your hands if it is easier. Shape spoonfuls of the mixture into crude balls, then roll each ball in extra ground nuts. Chill thoroughly and serve, and keep refrigerated between servings.

*Instead of ground nuts, you may roll the balls in fine shredded unsweetened coconut or sesame seeds.

Makes about 2 dozen.

Carob Fudge
(Prize-Winning Recipe)

E · G · S · Y · B · Gr

1 cup sesame tahini, peanut butter,
almond butter, cashew butter *or*
sunflower butter
1 cup honey*
1 cup sifted carob powder, dark roasted
2 Tbs. arrowroot powder

Use one or more of the following:
8–10 drops peppermint extract
1–2 tsp. real vanilla flavouring
⅛ – ½ tsp. orange, rum, lemon or other
flavouring

Stir the nut butter and honey over medium heat until softened, remove from heat, then mix in the remaining ingredients. Mix together well and press into a lightly oiled pan or pie plate. Chill thoroughly and cut into squares.

Or, the mixture may be semi-chilled, then rolled into little balls with raisin, date or nut centres and lastly rolled in coconut, sesame seeds or ground nuts.

Refrigerate between servings.

*Instead of 1 cup honey, you may use 1 cup fruit concentrate *or* ⅔ cup honey and ¼ cup maple syrup, *or* ¾ cup maple syrup and ¼ cup fruit juice (try orange, papaya, pear, peach or apple).

Nut Butter Balls E · G · Y · B · Gr · can be S

> ¾ cup peanut butter, sesame tahini,
> almond butter *or* cashew butter
> ¼ cup honey*
> ¼ cup instant soy milk powder *or* carob
> powder
> ¼ cup raisins, currants *or* chopped dried
> fruit*
> 2–3 dashes cinnamon
> *Optional:* whole almonds *or* cashews
> sesame seeds, shredded
> unsweetened coconut, ground
> nuts *or* seeds, for coating

Let the nut butter sit at room temperature for 10–20 minutes, then use a fork to mix it with the honey, soy milk powder or carob powder, dried fruit and cinnamon. Add a little extra soy milk powder or carob powder if harder nut balls are preferred.

Roll the mixture into bite-sized balls, around almond or cashew centres if desired. Then roll each ball in coconut or other coating. Chill before serving and refrigerate between servings.

*Instead of honey, you may use 3 Tbs. maple syrup, and decrease soy milk powder or carob powder to an equal amount. Instead of dried fruit, you may use chopped nuts, seeds *or* crispy brown rice cereal.

Fruit-Nut Candies   E · G · S · Y · B · Gr

1 cup very finely chopped dried fruit
(any combination of raisins,
currants, apricots, peaches,
pears, apples, dates, figs)
½–¾ cup ground nuts and/or seeds (any
combination of walnuts, pecans,
almonds, cashews, filberts
[hazelnuts], sunflower seeds,
pumpkin seeds, pine nuts)
honey, maple syrup *or* water
sesame seeds *or* shredded
unsweetened coconut

Mix the chopped dried fruit with the ground nuts (the fruit and
nuts can be ground separately in a food processor). Add a little
sweetener or water if the mixture is too dry. Shape the mixture
into balls, squares or other shapes, then roll them in sesame
seeds or coconut, pressing seeds gently into the surface. If the
coating does not stick well, roll the balls in a bit of sweetener
or water before rolling them again in the coconut or seeds. Chill
before serving and refrigerate between servings.
    Makes about 1 ½ dozen.

Gourmet Popcorn   E · G · S · B · can be Y

4 qts. freshly popped popcorn (about ½
cup corn)
4 Tbs. light, cold-pressed oil *or* clarified
butter
2–3 tsp. honey *or* 1–2 tsp. maple syrup
½ cup nutritional yeast, powdered*
seasoned or vegetable sea salt, to
taste

When the popcorn is popped and still hot, heat the oil until bubbly and stir in the sweetening. Pour it over the popcorn, spreading evenly. Immediately sprinkle on the yeast and salt. Mix well, serve and enjoy!

*Be sure to use *nutritional* yeast, as it has a nicer flavour. Instead of yeast and sea salt, you may use sesame salt (gomashio). (Yeast is *not* recommended for people with Candida).

Even people who don't like yeast find this popcorn delicious. It has a slight cheese flavour and is high in nutrients and B vitamins. Vary the seasonings to taste.

COOKIES

Pumpkin Cookies

G · Y · can be E · S

Dry ingredients:
2 cups millet flour*
½ cup soy flour, buckwheat flour *or*
amaranth flour
3 tsp. baking powder (wheat-free)
2 tsp. cinnamon
½ tsp. sea salt
½ tsp. nutmeg
¼ tsp. ginger
Optional: 1–2 cups raisins *or* currants
Optional: 1 cup chopped nuts

Wet ingredients:
½ cup light, cold-pressed oil
1 ¼ cups honey*
¾ cup brown date sugar *or* barley malt
powder *or* natural raw sugar
2 eggs, beaten*
Optional: 1 Tbs. molasses
Optional: 1–2 tsp. vanilla extract
1 ½ cups cooked, mashed pumpkin (see page
126)

Preheat the oven to 400–425°F. Stir the dry ingredients into
the wet. This makes a thick but pourable batter. Bake medium-
sized cookies for 12–14 minutes.

*Instead of honey, you may use 1 cup maple syrup and ¼ cup pumpkin liquid *or* water. Instead of millet flour, you may use 2 cups brown rice flour, *or* 1 cup brown rice flour and 1 cup millet flour. Egg substitutes may be used if desired. Makes 4–6 dozen.

Tapioca Treats   E · S · Y · B · can be Gr

¼ cup tapioca flour
¼ cup brown rice flour*
¼ cup barley malt powder*
3 Tbs. maple syrup
1 tsp. vanilla extract

½ cup crispy brown rice*
½ cup shredded unsweetened coconut*

Preheat the oven to 350°F. Combine the flours and malt powder and mix well. Add the maple syrup and vanilla extract and mix thoroughly. Carefully stir in the crispy brown rice, then mix in the coconut. Shape the mixture by teaspoonfuls into small balls, and flatten each to a thickness of about ⅜″ on lightly oiled cookie sheets. Bake for 8–10 minutes and remove them from the oven while they are still soft, but lightly browned. They will harden as they cool. Let them cool for about 30 minutes, then store in a tin with a small crust of bread inside to absorb excess moisture.

*You may try several variations on this recipe, all of which will slightly alter the flavour but not the consistency of the treats. Instead of rice flour, use millet flour. Instead of coconut, use ground nuts or seeds. Instead of crispy rice, use chopped nuts. Instead of barley malt powder, use *fine* brown date sugar (grind it in a blender, food processor or grinder) *or* natural raw sugar.

Note: This recipe should not be changed, except for the variations shown.

Makes 1½ dozen.

Tapioca Brittle E · S · Y · B

Preheat the oven to 400°F. Follow the directions for Tapioca Treats, above, but omit the rice flour and use only 2 Tbs. maple syrup. Flatten the balls to about ⅛″ thick and place them 1½–2″ apart on lightly oiled cookie sheets. Bake for 3–5 minutes until bubbling and a bit crispy. Remove from the oven, cool and store as for Tapioca Treats.

Note: Do not change the recipe for either Tapioca Treats or Tapioca Brittle, except for the suggested variations. Elimination of any one ingredient can spoil these recipes. Date sugar will not work in the Tapioca Brittle recipe, although it works in the Tapioca Treats recipe.

Walnut-Anise Cookies E · G · S · Y · B

½ cup honey*
¼ cup light, cold-pressed oil
¾ cup brown rice flour *or* millet flour
½ cup tapioca flour
¾ cup chopped walnuts
½ cup raisins, currants *or* chopped dates
¼ cup barley malt powder, brown date sugar *or* natural raw sugar
1 tsp. anise seeds
⅛ tsp. sea salt
Optional: ¼–½ cup shredded unsweetened coconut

Preheat the oven to 400°F. Mix the honey and oil together well. In a separate bowl, mix the remaining ingredients, then slowly mix them into the honey mixture. For each cookie, drop 1–2 Tbs. of the mixture on lightly oiled cookie sheets and bake 9–12 minutes, until lightly browned but still soft. Cool on wire racks.

*Instead of honey, you may use 6 Tbs. maple syrup and 2 Tbs. fruit juice, *or* ½–⅔ cup Date Spread (page 157).

Makes 1–1½ dozen.

"101" Cookies E · G · S · Y · can be Gr

Wet ingredients:
⅓ cup honey *or* maple syrup
¼ cup light, cold-pressed oil
1 Tbs. fruit juice (apple, pear, peach,
apricot, orange, papaya, etc.),
water *or* extra honey
1 tsp. vanilla extract

Dry ingredients:
¾ cup flour (brown rice flour, millet
flour, buckwheat flour, cassava
flour, amaranth flour, quinoa
flour or teff flour)
¼ cup powdered or granulated sweetener
¼ cup tapioca flour*
¼ cup arrowroot flour*
1 tsp. baking powder
½–1 tsp. cinnamon
⅛ tsp. sea salt

Preheat the oven to 375°F. Combine the wet ingredients thoroughly. In a separate bowl, sift together the dry ingredients. Add the dry ingredients to the wet and mix well. Drop by spoonfuls onto lightly oiled cookie sheets and flatten them to a thickness of ½″. Bake 12–14 minutes and let the cookies cool on wire racks. Store in a tin with a small crust of bread.

*Instead of ¼ cup tapioca flour and ¼ cup arrowroot powder, you may use ½ cup tapioca flour *or* ½ cup arrowroot powder.

This basic recipe makes 1–1½ dozen cookies. Choose your favourite variations to create dozens or delightful treats!

Fruit-Nut Cookies

Follow the directions for 101 Cookies, above, but add:
¼ cup raisins *or* currants
¼ cup chopped walnuts *or* pecans

Makes 1½–2 dozen.

Almond Cookies

Follow the directions for 101 Cookies, above, but omit:
1 Tbs. of the oil

and add:
¼ cup sliced or chopped almonds
2 Tbs. ground almonds
½–1 tsp. almond extract
the full 1 tsp. cinnamon in the basic recipe
1 Tbs. almond butter

Makes about 1½ dozen.

Orange or Lemon Cookies

Follow the directions for 101 Cookies, above, but omit:
1 Tbs. fruit juice

and add:
1 Tbs. orange or lemon juice
2 Tbs. finely grated orange or lemon rind
½–1 tsp. orange *or* lemon extract

Makes 1–1½ dozen.

Date Nut Cookies

Follow the directions for 101 Cookies, above, but omit:
    ⅓ cup honey
    ¼ cup granulated sweetener
    1 Tbs. fruit juice

and add:
    ½ cup Date Spread (page 157)
    ¼ cup brown date sugar *or* ¼ cup very
              finely chopped dried dates
  2-3 Tbs. fruit juice (lemon juice is best)
    ½ cup chopped filberts (hazelnuts),
              cashews *or* almonds

Makes about 1½ dozen.

Sesame Raisin Cookies

Follow the directions for 101 Cookies, above, but add:
    ¾ cup hulled sesame seeds
    ¼ cup raisins *or* currants

Makes about 2 dozen.

Pecan Cookies

Follow the directions for 101 Cookies, above, but omit:
    ¼ cup of the main flour

and add:
    ½ cup ground pecans
  ¼–½ cup chopped pecans

Press a half pecan into the centre of each cookie before baking.
Makes about 1½ dozen.

Double Carob Chip Cookies

Follow the directions for 101 Cookies, above, but omit:
¼ cup of the main flour

and add:
¼ cup carob powder, dark roasted
¼ – ½ cup carob chips

Makes about 1 ½ dozen.

Carrot Raisin Cookies

Follow the directions for 101 Cookies, above, but add:
½ cup finely grated carrot
¼ cup raisins *or* currants
1 Tbs. extra flour *or* powdered sweetener
the full 1 tsp. cinnamon in the basic recipe

Makes about 2 dozen.

Coconut Cookies

Follow the directions for 101 Cookies, above, but add:
½ – ¾ cup shredded unsweetened coconut
1 Tbs. coconut juice as the juice, if available

Makes 1 ½ – 2 dozen.

Peanut Butter Cookies

Follow the directions for 101 Cookies, above, but omit:
2–3 Tbs. of the oil

and add:
½ cup natural peanut butter
¼ cup raw chopped peanuts

Makes 1½–2 dozen.

Maple-Nut Cookies

Follow the directions for 101 Cookies, above, but add:
maple syrup rather than honey
½ cup chopped almonds, walnuts *or*
pecans
½–1 tsp. maple flavouring
2 tsp. vanilla extract (*additional*)
the full 1 tsp. cinnamon in the basic recipe

Makes 1½–2 dozen.

There are only 89 recipes to go — create your own!

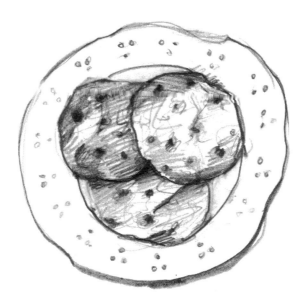

ICE CREAMS AND ICES · SYRUPS AND TOPPINGS

Important: When preparing ice cream, blend ingredients in *exactly the order given*, for a successful result. Nuts added to ice cream may be raw or roasted, as desired.

Dairy-Free Vanilla Ice Cream
G · Y · B · Gr

      2 eggs
  1 cup Cashew Milk #2 (page 32)
  4 Tbs. lecithin granules
  2 tsp. real vanilla flavouring
  ½ cup honey
  1 cup Cashew Milk #2

Use a blender to blend the eggs and add each ingredient, *in exactly the order given*, one by one, mixing well before adding the next ingredient. Freeze the mixture in a covered container. Homogenize the frozen mixture in a homogenizing juicer or food processor, then re-freeze it and enjoy.

Eat this ice cream just as it is, or serve it on cakes or pies or in beverages or milk shakes. It may also be prepared in an ice cream maker. Follow the manufacturer's instructions. Makes 1 quart.

Carob-Peppermint Ice Cream
G · Y · B · Gr

    1 egg
    1 cup Cashew Milk #2 (page 32)
    ½ cup carob powder
    4 Tbs. lecithin granules
    1¼ cups Cashew Milk #2
    1 tsp. real vanilla flavouring
    ½ tsp. peppermint extract
    ½ cup honey or other liquid sweetener

Follow the directions for Dairy-Free Vanilla Ice Cream, above.

Maple-Nut Ice Cream
G · Y · B · Gr

    2 eggs
    1 cup Cashew Milk #2 (page 32)
    4 Tbs. lecithin granules
    2 tsp. real vanilla flavouring
    6 Tbs. maple syrup
    1⅛ cup Cashew Milk #2
    ¼ tsp. real maple flavouring
    Optional: ½ cup chopped walnuts or pecans,
             raw or roasted

Follow the directions for Dairy-Free Vanilla Ice Cream,
above, but do not blend in the nuts. Stir them in just before the
second freezing.

Almond Ice Cream
G · Y · B · Gr

    2 eggs
    1 cup Almond Milk #2 (page 32) (or
             Cashew Milk #2, page 32)
    4 Tbs. lecithin granules
    2 tsp. real vanilla flavouring

½ cup honey
1 cup Almond Milk #2 *or* Cashew Milk #2
1 tsp. almond extract
½ cup finely chopped or slivered
      almonds, raw or roasted

Follow the directions for Dairy-Free Vanilla Ice Cream, above, but do not blend in the nuts. Stir them in just before the second freezing.

Frozen Ices   E · G · S · Y · B · Gr

Choose one or two fruits and freeze them solid for ices. Try berries, bananas, mangos, papaya, kiwi, pears, peaches, apricots, pineapple, citrus fruits, cherries, avocados, or other fruits suitable for freezing. Add just enough liquid sweetener or fruit juice to the frozen fruit so that it will blend or process easily and taste sweet enough for a dessert. Add a few dashes of sea salt, vanilla, rum, maple or other flavouring if desired. Freeze the mixture solid. Break the frozen mixture into chunks and soften with a food processor or homogenizing juicer. Freeze the mixture once again and enjoy! Hundreds of delightful, low-calorie ices can be prepared from this basic recipe.

Cup Pops   E · G · S · Y · B · Gr

1 cup fresh or frozen strawberries
1 medium banana, ripe
½ medium apple
5 Tbs. water

Blend or process all the ingredients together and freeze in small paper cups. Put a popsicle stick in the centre of each cup after the pop is partially frozen. When frozen, pull away the paper to enjoy a natural frozen pop. Make a variety of pops by trying other fruits and substituting fruit juice for the water.

Thanks to Viola Pilar for the original recipe for these treats.

Carob Fudge Topping

⅔ cup cashew milk, plain
⅓ cup honey *or* ¼ cup maple syrup (or
     less, to taste)
¼ cup carob powder, dark roasted
2 tsp. arrowroot powder
  dash sea salt
½ tsp. real vanilla flavouring

Blend all ingredients except the vanilla. Bring to a boil and simmer 5 minutes, stirring constantly, until the mixture thickens. Add vanilla. Remove from heat and serve hot or chilled, as a perfect finish for ice creams, cakes and other desserts.

Note: If you use vanilla extract instead of flavouring, it should be heated with the rest of the ingredients.

Carob Syrup

Follow the directions for Carob Fudge Topping, above, but omit the arrowroot powder. The mixture will thicken only slightly when heated. Use 3–4 Tbs. of cold syrup to flavour 1 cup of chilled milk substitute. Mix well before drinking. Delicious, especially in cold, plain, thick nut milk!

Applesauce

5–10 lbs. baking apples, including some
      · Spartan or MacIntosh
2–6 Tbs. water

Peel the apples. (Apple peels make the sauce bitter and require blending, which greatly reduces the flavour of the sauce. It is not worth using the apple peel unless the apples are organic. See Organic Applesauce, below.) Chop the apples into 1″ pieces and place them in a pot with a tight-fitting lid. Add 2–3 Tbs. water for every 5 lbs. apples. Turn the heat to high for *one minute only, staying close by the pot.* Turn the heat to low and simmer the apples for 30–60 minutes (depending on the amount used) or until they are tender enough to mash. Use a fine, small-holed hand masher and mash the apples well.

You may add cinnamon or sweetener if desired, but they are unnecessary if the apples have not been overcooked and if too much water has not been added.

Eat the applesauce hot or chill it for eating plain or with other foods. This is a delicious, naturally sweet side dish, snack or dessert. Can be served on top of ice cream too!

Organic Applesauce

Follow the directions for Applesauce, above, but use organic apples. Wash the apples and cut off any blemishes on the skin, but do not peel them. Remove the cores and chop in 1″ pieces. Cook as directed, cool the apples and blend in a blender, a small amount at a time, until smooth, or use a food processor.

A bit of sweetening, cinnamon and a dash of sea salt may be added to enhance the flavour of the applesauce.

Sweet Cranberry Sauce
E · G · S · Y · B · Gr

½ lb. fresh *or* frozen cranberries
1 cup water
¼ – ½ cup honey *or* maple syrup (or to taste)

Wash the cranberries, then put them in a pan with the water, cover and simmer over low heat for 12–20 minutes, or until the berries break down and mix with the water. When the cooking is done and the sauce is still hot, add the sweetening to taste.

Chill thoroughly before using. For a finer sauce, blend or strain this sauce.

Serve with breads, poultry, legumes (beans), or serve it on cakes and ice creams (see page 152).

Date Spread or Topping

1–1¼ lbs. (500 g) pitted dates
⅔ cup water
several dashes sea salt

Optional:
2 Tbs. lemon juice
1–2 Tbs. finely grated lemon rind

Put all ingredients in a saucepan and cook on low to medium-low heat until the dates are soft and mix easily with the water. When the mixture can be stirred into a pastelike texture, take it off the heat and let it cool before using.

Use Date Spread in place of jam, as a honey substitute, in Date Squares (page 138), or as a topping on ice creams or other desserts.

Fruit Butter or Topping

½ cup dried apricots, pears *or* peaches,
finely chopped
½ cup water

Combine the ingredients in a covered saucepan. Bring to a boil, then simmer for 15 minutes over low heat. Turn off heat and let stand, covered, 30 minutes or longer. The fruit absorbs more water as it cools. Add extra water or juice as necessary. Keep refrigerated between servings.

This chunky spread is a great sweetener on pancakes, cereals and ice creams. Experiment by substituting it for other sweeteners in breads and cookies.

The mixture can be stirred to soften it, or blended or mixed in a food processor to make a smoother, more spreadable topping. Prepared this way, it can be used as a sandwich spread instead of honey or jelly.

Strawberry Topping E · G · S · Y · B · Gr

½ lb. fresh or frozen strawberries*
1 cup water
2–3 Tbs. arrowroot powder
2–5 Tbs. liquid sweetener

Heat the strawberries in ½ cup of the water and mash them as they heat (or slice them before heating). Mix the remaining ½ cup water thoroughly with the arrowroot powder. Add the arrowroot mixture and sweetener to the strawberries and stir constantly over medium heat until the sauce becomes bright red and thickens. Chill and serve with Tofu Cheesecake (page 138), ice creams (page 152) or other desserts. Keeps 7–8 days in the refrigerator.

*Instead of strawberries, you may use blackberries, raspberries, blueberries, peach slices or other fruit.

Tofu Whipped Cream E · G · Y · B · Gr

6–8 oz. very fresh soft or regular plain tofu
(do *not* use pressed, flavoured
varieties or Japanese tofu, and
do *not* use tofu that has been
previously frozen)
4–5 Tbs. maple syrup, or to taste
1–2 tsp. real vanilla flavouring
Optional: 1–2 dashes cinnamon

Rinse the tofu in cold water and press between several layers of paper towels to squeeze out all water possible. Break the tofu into small pieces or mash it, and put it in the blender or food processor. Add the remaining ingredients and blend. Taste and adjust flavouring if desired, then blend again if necessary. Chill and serve.

Tofruity Whipped Cream

E · G · Y · B · Gr

Follow the directions for Tofu Whipped Cream, above, but add ¼ cup fruit jam or spread.

INFORMATION FOR THE COOK

STORAGE CHART

These foods can be safely stored as shown, if wrapped carefully, stored exactly as directed and kept bacteria-free. Store in jars, tins or plastic containers, up to the time shown in the left-hand column.

Refrigerate

6 months	rice polish
3–6 months	eggs
2 weeks	tofu
6 months	baking yeast
3 months	products containing natural oils that are not in airtight containers
2 weeks	nut milks & soy milk in liquid form
6 months–2 years	pitted dates
6 months–2 years	dried apricots
2 weeks	candies and cakes
2 weeks	cooked cereals

Refrigerate or keep in cool, dry place

1–several years	amaranth grain
6 months	dried fruits
Several years	whole grains

Several years	legumes—beans, peas, lentils (don't refrigerate)
3 months	granola and muesli
6 months–2 years	dried coconut
3–6 months	raw nuts and seeds
6 months–2 years	barley malt powder
1–several years	tamari soy sauce
2 weeks	breads

Store on shelf

Several years	carob powder
Several years	honey
Several years	herbs and spices
Several years	arrowroot powder
Several years	agar agar
Several years	sea kelp and sea salt
3 months	baking powder
6 months	soy milk powder
6 months–2 years	cream of tartar
6 months–2 years	baking soda
6 months–2 years	guar gum
6 months–2 years	xanthan gum
6 months	apple cider vinegar
3 months	boxed and puffed cereals
3 months–2 years	pharmacy powders
6 months–2 years	vitamin C crystals
3–6 months	packaged mixes
3–6 months	crackers and rice cakes

Store on shelf 1 year or less, refrigerate when opened

3 months	natural oil
3 months	natural mayonnaise
3 months	natural ketchup

3–6 months	natural peanut butter
3–6 months	sesame tahini
3 months	other nut butters
2 weeks	fruit butters
3 months	natural jams and jellies
1–2 years	real maple syrup
1–2 years	liquid lecithin
1–2 years	lecithin granules
3 months	barley malt liquid

Freeze

3 months	ice creams and ices
3 months	millet breads
6 months	leftover legumes and tofu
6 months	leftover sauces and gravies
6 months–2 years	millet flour

Freeze if possible, or keep cool

6 months–2 years	amaranth flour
6 months	all other flours
3 months	breads (if frozen)
6 months	cornmeal

FOOD GLOSSARY

Agar agar. A jelling agent or thickener, made from a clear, white seaweed, often used instead of gelatin. It must be heated and stirred into a liquid until no longer "grainy." It should be strained unless it came in powder form. Does not work well when used with cirtus juices.

Almonds and almond milk. High in protein, calcium and fats. One of many good dairy substitutes.

Amaranth (seed, flour or puffed). Made from the grain-like seed of a tall plant native to Mexico, but now grown in the U.S. and a little bit in eastern Canada. The ancient Aztecs were nourished on this high-energy food, which is a complete protein and high in calcium and other nutrients. This is *not* a grain. Use it in grain-free baking recipes with tapioca, arrowroot or other starchy flours to lighten baked goods made with amaranth. Amaranth has a robust, pleasant, nut-like flavour. For more information, write Amaranth Information, Rodale Press, 33 E. Miner St., Emmaus PA USA 18049.

Amazake. Rice culture sweetener made from koji (aspergillus oryzae) added to rice. It is easy to digest and a mild but flavourful sweetener usually found in liquid form. Use in place of honey or maple syrup in recipes. For 1 cup maple syrup, use ½–¾ cup amazake and extra liquid or juice to equal 1 cup.

Arrowroot powder or flour. From the dried root of a tropical plant. Arrowroot, which is in a food family by itself, is a thickening agent that may be used in place of cornstarch, in about the same quantity. Unlike cornstarch, arrowroot is wholesome, easily tolerated and will not contribute to constipation, diarrhea or vitamin loss in the body. It is an important ingredient in egg-free recipes.

Baking powder. See page 20.

Baking soda. The alkaline ingredient used in many baking powders.

Baking yeast. A living fungus (before baking) used to leaven breads and some baked goods. 1 Tbs. equals 1 packet or square of yeast. Avoid brands that contain chemicals or preservatives like BHA and BHT.

Barley. Pot barley is a whole grain used in main dishes and soups. Barley flour is also available, but is one of the four high-gluten grains. See also *Job's tears*.

Barley malt (powder or syrup). Used as a mild sweetening agent. Good for wheat-free diets, but it does contain gluten.

Besan. See *chick pea flour*.

Buckwheat (grain and flour). This grain has wheat in its name, but it has nothing to do with wheat and is gluten-free. For some reason, however, about 50% of people who cannot tolerate gluten also cannot tolerate buckwheat. Whole grain buckwheat makes a tasty main dish. The flour is dark and has a robust, slightly sweet flavour. Use ¼ to 1 cup in recipes. See also *kasha*.

Butters (nut and fruit). Nut butters are nuts or seeds ground into a spread like peanut butter or sesame butter. Fruit butters are puréed fruits.

Calcium carbonate. An alkaline ingredient sometimes used in baking powder recipes instead of baking soda.

Calcium phosphate. An acidic ingredient sometimes used in baking powder recipes instead of cream of tartar.

Carob (powder/flour and pods). A chocolate substitute from the legume family. Dark roasted carob powder tastes more like chocolate. Raw, light carob tastes more fruity. It contains ten times less fat and many fewer calories than its equivalent, cocoa powder. The roasted pods have a pleasant, malt-like flavour, and they are crunchy and fun to chew on. Eat all but the seeds. Unlike chocolate, carob is caffeine-free and does not hinder the absorption of calcium as chocolate does. If you are allergic to carob but can tolerate chocolate, use unsweetened cocoa powder in place of carob powder in equal quantities. Don't use chocolate squares, chunks or powder for a carob powder substitute, as they will make the foods too sweet.

Cashews and cashew milk. Nuts high in calcium, protein and fats. One of many good dairy substitutes.

Cassava flour or root. From a starchy tropical root vegetable which is also the main source of tapioca. The pre-cooked woody root is also available frozen and may be boiled and mashed like potatoes.

Cayenne pepper. A natural red pepper, ground and dried, used for seasoning main dishes and vegetables. This is not a spice, and though it appears to be hotter and stronger than black pepper, it is actually milder for the stomach and more digestible. Cayenne pepper has been shown to help break up mucus and cholesterol in the body, and may contribute to improved circulation. Mild, medium and hot cayenne are available, but not always labelled, so experiment with amounts. Use about ⅛–¼ tsp. cayenne instead of 1 tsp. white or black pepper. If you are allergic to cayenne pepper, use black or white pepper, as little as possible.

Chana flour. Chick pea flour or besan.

Cheese. As a substitute, use tofu or tofu cheeses in many recipes. Nutritional yeast may also be used in mock cheese recipes. See *tofu cheese, nutritional yeast* and *goat cheese*.

Chick peas (garbanzo beans). A main dish legume (bean) that when cooked properly is more easily digested than most beans. High in protein, calcium, iron, phosphorus, potassium and other nutrients. Chick peas contain more calcium than many dairy products and make a good dairy substitute.

Chick pea flour (besan, chana). A bit (¼–½ cup per recipe) can be used to add protein to bread recipes. Used commonly in East Indian foods like chipatis.

Cilantro. Mexican or Chinese parsley.

Coconut. A tropical fruit. Dried, unsweetened coconut is used in many of the recipes in this book, usually fine grated or fine shredded. Avoid sweetened coconut, which contains a large amount of sugar. The coconut is quite sweet all by itself. Coconut milk can be used as a milk substitute (see pages 33 and 34).

Corn flour. Many brands contain wheat and should be avoided. Find a pure, fine-ground corn flour for use in recipes, and make sure it is *whole* grain corn flour.

Cornmeal. A whole grain. Medium, not coarse ground, is best used for breakfast cereal or bread recipes. Corn and corn products of all types are often difficult to digest for those with food sensitivities.

Cornstarch. See *arrowroot*.

Cream of tartar. An acidic ingredient used in baking powder.

Crispy brown rice cereal. A tasty, wheat-free cereal. It usually contains barley malt, which contains gluten. It is a nice addition to some cookie and cake recipes and may even be sprinkled on desserts as a topping.

Dairy substitutes. These include high-protein, high-calcium foods like tofu, chick peas, pinto beans, black beans, sesame seeds and tahini, cashews and almonds. These foods may also mock the flavour, colour and texture of some dairy products. Nutritional yeast mocks the flavour but not the nutrients of dairy foods.

Date sugar. A coarse *brown* sugar made from dates. It is not heavily sweet, but adds good flavour and consistency to cakes and cookies when used with a second sweetening agent like honey or maple syrup.

Eggs. Buy free-range or organic eggs when possible. Duck, quail or other eggs can sometimes be tolerated by people who cannot eat hen's eggs. One hen's egg is about ¼ cup liquid, so measure other eggs accordingly. See About Eggs (page 28).

Egg substitutes. Various substitutes are shown in each recipe. Packaged egg substitutes may also be used. See the Buying Guide (page 177) and Tip #1 about eggs in Important Tips on Baking Breads (page 18) and About Eggs (page 28).

Flax seed (linseed). Add to cooked cereals whole or ground. The seed has a strong flavour, is high in nutrients, is good for strong hair and nails and has a mild laxative effect. Ground flax can also be added to dry cereals (¼–1 tsp.) or breads (1–3 tsp.) for extra nutrients. Flax seeds can be used to make an egg substitute (see page 28).

Fruit, dried. High in iron and natural sugars. Choose un-sulphured varieties, as sulphur has been known to agitate the liver and kidneys and to affect the digestion of those with food sensitivities.

Fruit concentrate. May be used in place of honey or maple syrup, in about equal proportions. This specially manufactured sweetener is a highly concentrated fruit product not to be confused with *fruit juice concentrate*. It equals other liquid sweeteners in its ability to flavour desserts and other recipes.

Fruit juice. May be used as a sole sweetening agent in some recipes, with some variation in flavour. For example, if a recipe calls for 2 cups honey and 1½ cups nut milk, use 3½ cups of a thick variety of peach or pear juice (other fruit juices are not as sweet or light coloured). The recipe can be made sweeter by replacing ½ cup or so of the flour for the same amount of powdered or granulated sweetener.

Fruit juice concentrate. Frozen and bottled concentrated juices or fruit juice syrups. These may be used to sweeten some recipes but are not equivalent to other liquid sweeteners and must be experimented with.

Garbanzo beans and flour. See *chick peas*.

Gluten grains and flours. Technically speaking, all true grains contain at least a small amount of gluten. However, most people allergic to gluten grains can tolerate everything except the four high-gluten grains: wheat, rye, barley and oats. Spelt and kamut also contain more gluten but are more digestible for some individuals with food sensitivities. See *kamut* and *spelt*.

Gluten-free grains and flours. Grains containing only minute amounts of gluten. These include buckwheat (kasha), rice, millet, quinoa and corn.

Goat cheese (and milk). 50% or more of people who are allergic to cow's milk products can tolerate goat dairy products. Goat milk is closer to human milk in quality, and is easier to digest and generally lower in fats and cholesterol. See your doctor and experiment with goat yogurt, milk and cheeses. Goat products are usually mild in flavour if the goat keepers keep the male goats separate from the female.

Gomashio. See *sesame salt*.

Grain-free flours. Those who cannot eat any grains should use carob, amaranth, arrowroot, nut, tapioca, teff, cassava and potato flours to add bulk and starch to their diets. Legume (bean) flours such as soy flour, lentil flour or chick pea flour are also grain-free. See Homemade Flours, page 19. Those with grain allergies should use grain-free flours and eat more starchy vegetables like squash, potatoes, cauliflower, turnips, parsnips and carrots.

Grains, whole. The small, hard seeds of a cereal grass. Whole grains or starches are a nutritious and essential part of everyone's diet. See also *grain-free flours*.

Guar gum powder. A thickener and binder used to help gluten-free baked goods keep their rise. Derived from a nutritious East Indian seed, guar gum can be used in place of eggs or liquid lecithin, but should not be used in yeast breads. It is good for peptic ulcers and is used as a mild laxative and appetite suppressant. Use small amounts only.

Gums. See *guar gum powder* and *xanthan gum*.

Hato mugi. See *Job's tears*.

Honey. A liquid sweetener gathered and processed by bees from flower nectars. There are many varieties and flavours, with varying mineral content. Choose a good-flavoured, high-quality honey for eating and cooking. Those with allergies should avoid *raw* honey except for cooking. Pasteurizing honey destroys bacteria, enzymes and nutrients but is safer for sensitive people. Babies under two years old should never be given raw honey, as it is claimed that raw honey can contribute to crib death.

Honeyleaf (also called stevia, sweet leaf and sweet herb). A potent South American herb sweetener. A few drops are as sweet as tablespoons of other liquid sweeteners. It mixes easily with hot or cold foods and has one-three-hundredth the calories of sugar. Experiment with it in beverages, breads and desserts. About 1–3 drops sweetens 1 cup liquid.

Job's tears (hato mugi) Although it is sometimes called pearl barley, this unique grain is nothing like the small, white, round, refined pearl barley available in many stores. It is not really barley at all. It looks somewhat like puffed brown rice and is the seed of an annual wild grass. This biblically named seed has been used for thousands of years. One macrobiotic sourcebook claims Job's tears will counteract the effect of eating animal proteins and fats, and that it is a cooling food, good for cancers and other growths like warts and moles. Use the seed in soups and stews or with brown rice instead of barley. It is a robust seed with a pungent flavour.

Juices. Choose natural, unsweetened, pure fruit juices for use in recipes. Avoid those with artificial flavours and colours.

Kamut (pronounced "ka-moot") (grain or flour). A Mediterranean, unhybridized wheat, which until recently has been almost ignored in favour of commercial quality wheat. Interest in the grain has been revived because many people allergic to common wheat can tolerate kamut with no allergic reaction (*if you have a severe wheat allergy, check with your doctor before trying kamut*). This may be because kamut has not been as overprocessed as common wheat. Therefore, it contains 40% more protein and 65% more amino acids, and it is more digestible. Kamut also has a superior flavour—slightly sweet and nut-like. Use this large, soft, white wheat in cooking and baking, as successfully as wheat. Kamut is a good pasta grain as well.

Kasha. This is buckwheat grain, lightly toasted until it is brown in colour. It makes a main dish more tasty, as it has a nut-like flavour.

Kelp powder (sea kelp). A ground seaweed containing iodine. Adds flavour and minerals to many foods. This is an important ingredient to the flavour of many main dishes, especially the paté, bean dishes and tomato sauce.

Kidney beans. Oval-shaped red beans (legumes), high in flavour and nutrients. Use them in chilis and stews. For some, these are less digestible than pinto beans or chick peas.

Kudzu powder (kuzu). A starch-like extract of a Japanese root that comes in crumbly white chunks. It is used as an arrowroot-like thickener or gelling agent like agar agar, and is prized for its medicinal and healing effects. In Asia, the chopped root is used for tea and the powder is made into noodles. It is also a plentiful weed in the southern U.S.

Lecithin (granules or liquid). A soy product that acts as a binder and *natural* preservative. It also helps control cholesterol levels. Add granules to cooked foods or ice cream recipes. Use the liquid in energy protein drinks and baked foods. The liquid is *very* sticky and should be handled carefully. When measuring it into mixtures, judge the quantity by eye rather than actually measuring. It won't matter if you are off by a teaspoon.

Lecithin spread. A processed margarine or butter substitute with a rather "filmy," oily taste. Some tolerate its flavour while others find it necessary to mask it in other recipes, like the delicious Veggie Butter (page 67).

Legumes. Includes beans, peas and lentils. Legumes are high in protein and low in fat (cholesterol-free), and some are high in calcium, iron and other nutrients as well. They are an important food and very digestible *if* cooked correctly. See How to Cook Beans Properly (page 26).

Legume flours. Non-grain, high-protein flours that include soy and chick pea flours.

Lentils (brown). A quick-cooking legume that makes a nice main dish. It does not need pre-soaking. Also called green or grey lentils.

Maple syrup. The boiled sap of maple trees. A very sweet and flavourful sweetener that can replace honey in many recipes. Use ½–¾ cup maple syrup in place of 1 cup honey, and substitute the remaining ¼–½ cup liquid with juice or water. Maple syrup is usually sweeter than honey, but more expensive. Use 100% pure maple syrup,

#1 or A grade for the best flavour. Medium or B or C grades are higher in nutrients, but not sweet enough for recipes. Use these grades for medicinal purposes, cleansing or beverages.

Milk substitutes. Includes nut, seed and/or soy milks. Choose any of them when a recipe calls for milk substitute. Buy them at the store or make them at home (see page 31). *Experiment* with using vegetable milks (Zucchini Milk, page 35 and Alfalfa Milk, page 35) in recipes.

Millet. A tasty, nutritious, gluten-free whole-grain cereal or main dish grain that is very alkaline. Good for children and people with delicate stomachs. Even people with rice allergies can often tolerate millet. It is higher in nutrients than many grains, including brown rice. Delicious!

Millet flour. A slightly heavy, somewhat bitter flour unless balanced with other flavours, such as milk substitute, juice or sweeteners. Cinnamon or allspice in a recipe also offsets the bitterness. A *good* main flour for those with gluten allergies. Best if kept frozen.

Molasses. The nutritious part of heated sugar cane syrup. The best varieties are not sugar by-products. A rich, dark, heavy-tasting sweetener, molasses is overpowering to some people, pleasant to others. It is high in iron. Buy unsulphured, Barbados varieties for cooking. Blackstrap molasses is full of nutrients but is too strong-tasting for most people. Some varieties (cooking molasses, table molasses and sulphured) contain wheat — check the label to make sure.

Nut milks. Dairy-free milk substitutes made from nuts like almonds and cashews (see page 31).

Nutritional yeast. Varieties include brewer's, torula, primary and engevita yeast. They may be eaten as they are purchased or used in cooking to help create mock cheese flavours. They are high in many nutrients, especially B vitamins. Brewer's and torula yeasts are often used in blended protein drinks, while engevita and primary golden powder or flaked varieties are more often used in cooking and work best in the recipes in this book. Those with Candida and certain other allergies should avoid all types of yeast. Nutritional yeasts are not leavened yeasts to be used in baking!

Nuts, raw. Generally more nutritious and flavourful than toasted nuts. The best ones contain no preservatives. Your health food store will probably have the freshest ones. Chew them very well for the best digestibility.

Oat flour. A gluten flour good for wheat-free and rye-free diets. This is a good-flavoured, medium-heavy flour and can be substituted for wheat in many recipes.

Oats, rolled. Raw, pressed, flattened whole oats that cook quickly. Use for cereals, breads and dessert recipes.

Oats, whole. A whole grain containing gluten. Use for cereals or main dishes, for people with wheat-free diets.

Oils. Use natural oils (made without chemicals) for most recipes in this book. Choose light-coloured and light-flavoured, cold-pressed oils for most of these recipes. Sunflower, safflower, sesame and nut-derived oils are among the best varieties for bread and dessert recipes.

Onions. As an onion substitute, 1 tsp. prepared horseradish = approximately ⅓–½ cup chopped onion. You may want to increase the herbs and spices too.

Pepper. See *cayenne pepper*.

Pinto beans. Brown-flecked, cream-coloured beans. They are easier to digest than many other beans. Use them in Mexican dishes. They are especially high in calcium and minerals.

Potassium bicarbonate. Low-sodium baking soda.

Potato flour. A starchy, mild-tasting flour. A good thickener and binder, it expands more than other flours. It usually turns orange when cooked by itself or with oil, but retains its colour if baked with other gluten-free flours.

Quinoa (pronounced "keen-wah"). A quick-cooking, essentially gluten-free, high-protein grain, excellent for allergy diets. The "mother grain of the Incas" is grown in South and North America. It is not a true grain, but is excellent used in place of rice or millet as a cereal or main-dish grain.

Rice (brown and wild). High-nutrient, essentially gluten-free whole grains, available in short and long grain varieties. Rice makes a wonderful main dish. Wild rice is tastiest with its rich, robust flavour and even higher in nutrients than other rice varieties. Sweet brown rice is great for breakfast cereals and rice pudding.

Rice flour. A mild, very light flour that does not bind well without other flours or starches, eggs or other binder. It is a good "gluten-free" main flour that comes in whole grain brown rice flour *or* white rice flour. Brown is preferable.

Rolled rice and barley. Sometimes available in health food stores. Use instead of rolled oats in some recipes.

Rye flour. A heavy, dark, strong-flavoured flour containing gluten. It is rarely used by itself. Recipes for rye bread are usually ¼ to ½ rye, plus other flours.

Sea kelp. See *kelp*.

Sea salt. Derived from vacuum-dried seawater and containing the natural minerals usually refined out of earth salt. It is easier to digest than earth salt and contains no chemicals or sugar. It is not always iodized, however, so sea kelp is a necessary diet supplement. Because sea salt is saltier than other table salt, use ⅔ ¾ tsp sea salt in place of 1 tsp. salt. Vegetable sea salt has dried, ground vegetables like spinach, celery, watercress and carrot added to flavour and extend the sea salt, while adding extra nutrients.

Sesame butter. See *sesame tahini*.

Sesame milk. A seed milk, and a high-calcium dairy substitute.

Sesame salt (gomashio). A mixture of 4–10 parts toasted ground sesame seeds and 1 part sea salt. Toast hulled sesame seeds on a flat, dry pan in a 350°F oven for 8–14 minutes, stirring once or twice, until browned.

Sesame tahini. A peanut-butter-like food made from hulled, ground sesame seeds with oil added. Tahini is a good protein and calcium supplement for dairy-free diets. Roasted, hulled sesame seeds make the most flavourful tahini. Sesame butter is made from *un*hulled, ground sesame seeds, has a bit stronger flavour and is sometimes a bit harder to digest.

Sodium bicarbonate. Another name for baking soda.

Sorghum. A syrup made from a grain similar to Indian corn. It is largely unrefined and used as a natural sweetener, especially in the southern U.S.

Spelt (grain or flour). A European grain closely related to wheat. Nicknamed "dinkle," spelt has a high gluten content. It can be substituted for wheat in any recipe, with the same results in texture and taste. Many people who cannot tolerate wheat can eat spelt, but *check with your doctor first*. Spelt looks and cooks like wheat, but is softer and redder in colour. It contains more protein (balanced amino acids), fats and crude fibre than common wheat, and it is more easily digested. Use a bit less liquid or more flour when using spelt in place of wheat in recipes. Spelt is also a good pasta grain.

Stevia. See *honeyleaf*.

Sugar, raw. Real, true raw sugar is currently made only in Europe. It is available under the brand name SUCANAT® (from SUgar CAne NATural). Most other "raw" sugars are refined white sugars with molasses and other colouring additives included, then crystallized in various consistencies. SUCANAT is less sweet than regular sugar and more sweet than brown date sugar or barley malt powder. In recipes, try 1¼–1¾ cups SUCANAT in place of 1 cup sugar, and decrease the dry ingredients accordingly. In place of ½ cup brown date sugar or barley malt powder, use ¼–⅓ cup SUCANAT and enough extra flour or other dry ingredient to equal ½ cup. Liquid sweeteners can also be used instead, with a little more adjusting.

Tahini. See *sesame tahini*.

Tamari. Naturally fermented soy sauce. Supermarket tamari can contain chemical additives and most kinds of tamari contain wheat, so shop carefully (see the Buying Guide, page 177, for wheatless and low-salt tamari). For salt-free diets, try Bernard Jensen's Quick Sip instead of tamari. Those on soy-free diets might experiment with Worcestershire sauce as a substitute in some recipes. Tamaris vary in thickness; use extra tamari in recipes if needed.

Tapioca flour. A gluten-free, grain-free flour usually derived from cassava root. Tapioca is a starchy, slightly sweet, white, powder like flour. Use about ¼–1 cup per recipe to sweeten rice and millet flour breads, and especially for sweet desserts.

Tartaric acid. An acidic ingredient sometimes used with another acidic ingredient in baking powders, along with an alkaline ingredient.

Teff (grain or flour). An Ethiopian grain whose name translates as "lost," a consequence of dropping this smallest of grains. One grain of wheat weighs the same as about 150 grains of teff. The grain ranges in colour from ivory or tan to brown and reddish varieties. It contains five times the iron, calcium and potassium of any other grain, is high in protein and fibre and is gluten-free. Teff has been used for thousands of years to bake Injera, a delicious Ethiopian flat bread. Use teff as a cereal or in cookies, burgers or main dishes. ½ cup of whole teff can also be used like 1 cup sesame seeds in cooked or baked recipes.

Tofu. A soy product made from pressed soy flour and water. Tofu is high in calcium, phosphorous and potassium. It makes a good cheese substitute in dairy-free diets. See About Tofu (page 30) for more information.

Tofu cheese. A basically non-dairy cheese substitute available in cheddar, mozzarella, Monterey jack and jalapeño flavours. Great for dairy-free diets, except they may contain casein, a protein dairy derivative. See the Buying Guide (page 177) for brand names.

Vitamin C crystals. An acidic ingredient used instead of cream of tartar to help baked goods rise. See "Add to Recipe" Baking Powders, page 23.

Water. Those with allergies should avoid drinking tap water and instead drink distilled water or water filtered by reverse osmosis. Sparkling bottled waters should generally be avoided as the minerals they contain can contribute to constipation. Club soda is a better sparkling water substitute for most, as it tends to loosen the bowels.

Xanthan gum. A *corn*-derived thickener and emulsifier. It improves the texture of baking powder breads and acts as a good binder and thickening agent in puddings and dressings. Also used in the packaging of meat and poultry.

Yeast. See *baking yeast* and *nutritional yeast*.

Zucchini (courgette, marrow). A green summer squash, delicious raw or cooked and very digestible. It can be made into milk (see page 35).

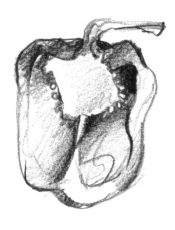

BUYING GUIDE

Part 1

These items are available from average retail stores, including pharmacies, markets and specialty stores. They may be purchased by individual consumers and usually do not require special ordering.

Available at some pharmacies:
    Calcium phosphate, potassium bicarbonate, tartaric acid, calcium carbonate or phosphate, vitamin C crystals (make sure they are pure and corn-free, if you are allergic to corn)

Available at supermarkets:
    Baking soda, cream of tartar, some soy products, some rice products, arrowroot (it is not recommended you buy arrowroot here, though — small amounts cost up to ten times what health food stores charge!), some gluten-free cereals, crackers or flour products, corn products, rice cakes, puffed cereals, honey.

Available at health food stores:
    Gluten-free flours, noodles, crackers, breads, mixes, cereals, lecithin, dairy and egg substitutes, arrowroot, agar agar, barley malt, oils, sweeteners, pure juices, vitamin C crystals, grains, raw nuts, nut butters, unsulphured dried fruits, free-range eggs, guar gum, legumes (beans and peas), soy products, tamari, carob, dairy-free ice creams, rice cakes, puffed cereals.

Available at some East Indian specialty stores:
    Gluten-free flours, papadams, chick pea flours (also called chana or besan), grains, herbs and spices.

Available at most Chinese specialty stores:
    Mung noodles, rice crackers and products, rice wrappers, various flours.

Available at most Mexican specialty stores:
Beans, corn products — flours, breads, corn chips.

Part 2

These special items *cannot* be ordered directly by individuals. Ask your favourite health food store to order them from these wholesale suppliers, which may have more local distributors closer to your area. Only a few of the major products available from the suppliers are listed here. If these food items cannot be ordered through your local store, see Available retail/wholesale by mail order (page 182).

Available in Canadian stores:

1. Artesian Acres
   R.R. #3, Lacombe, Alberta T0C 1F0
   Organic quinoa and kamut grain, flours and pasta.

2. Bio Option (Bioforce)
   4001 Cote Vertu, St-Laurent PQ H4R 1R5
   Wheat- and yeast-free vegetable broth powder, soy and vegetable bouillon cubes, soy milks, rice cakes.

3. Canasoy Enterprises Ltd.
   57 Lakewood, Vancouver BC V5L 4W4
   Gluten-free flours, noodles, mixes, milk and egg substitutes, oils, arrowroot, lecithin granules and liquid, lecithin spread, barley malt powder and liquid, barley, oat and tapioca flours, rice crackers.

4. Del Bonita Natural Products Ltd.
   P.O. Box 38, Stn. G, Calgary AB T3A 2G1
   Spelt grain and pasta.

5. Flora Distributing
   7400 Fraser Park Dr., Burnaby BC V5J 5B9
   Organic cold-pressed oils, rice snacks, Sucanat® raw sugar

6. Horizon Distributors
   3450 Vanness, Vancouver BC V5R 5A9
   (Serves Western Canada only, including Manitoba)
   Whole grains and legumes, quinoa, spelt, kamut, gluten-free flours, seeds, agar agar, kudzu, nut butters, soy products, tofu cheese (Tofurella), brown rice syrup, barley malt, rice and corn pasta, wheat-free tamari, rice crackers. (Organic whenever possible.)

7. Liv-N-Well Distributors Ltd.
   7591 Barkerville Crt., Richmond BC V7A 1K8
   Canadian distributors for Ener-G Foods Inc. (see products listed under U.S. stores).

8. Maximum Nutrition
   285 Nantucket Blvd., Scarborough ON M1P 2P2 *or*
   780 Place Trans Canada, Longueil PQ J4G 1P1
   Nutri-Max products, gluten-free flours, whole grains, nuts and nut butters, condiments, carob, quinoa.

9. Nationwide Natural Foods (and Lifestream Products)
   9451 Van Horne Way, Richmond BC V6X 1W2
   Barley malt liquid, oils, nut butters, gluten-free flours, grains, carob, soy products.

10. Northern Lights Wild Rice, Inc.
    P.O. Box 480, LaRonge SK S0J 1L0
    Wild rice and a variety of wild rice flour pastas.

11. Pastariso Products Inc.
    55 Ironside Crescent, Unit 6 & 7, Scarborough ON M1X 1N3
    Brown rice flour pastas, rice products

12. Purity Life Health Products Ltd.
    West: 313–8495 Ontario St., Vancouver BC V5X 3E8
    East: 100 Elgin St. S., Acton ON L7J 2W1
    Gluten-free snacks, cookies and candies, brown rice pasta and crackers, wild rice pasta, soy products, soy margarine, macrobiotic foods, cereals, blue corn, wheat-free tamari,

nut butters (including macadamia, pecan, filbert, sesame and sunflower), honeyleaf sweetener (stevia).

13. Tundra Wild Rice, Inc.
P.O. Box 263, Pine Falls MB R0E 1M0
Wild rice and wild rice flour.

14. Vita Health Co. Ltd.
150 Beghin Ave., Winnipeg MB R2J 8W2
Spelt, kamut, whole grains and legumes, nuts and seeds, soy and almond butters, oils, soy products, seaweeds, lecithin spreads.

Available in Canadian and U.S. stores:

1. Arrowhead Mills, Inc.
P.O. Box 2059, Hereford TX 79045
All organic whole grains and legumes, nut butters and condiments, teff, gluten-free products and flours.

2. Debole's Nutritional Food Inc.
Garden City Park NY 11040, USA
Corn pasta: spaghetti, lasagne, ribbons, macaroni, shells.

3. Eden Food Inc.
701 Tecumseh Rd., Clinton MI 49236, USA
Soy milk and soy products, wheat-free tamari, shoyu, unsweetened applesauce and other condiments.

4. Erewhon, Inc.
Wilmington MA 01887, USA
Cereals, rice crackers, snacks, barley malt candies, oils, unsweetened applesauce, nut butters

5. Knudsen's (R. W. & Sons, Inc.)
Chico CA 95926, USA
Unsweetened fruit juices, jams, fruit syrups.

6. Moore's Flour Mill
Milwaukie OR 97222, USA
Gluten-free flours, baking mixes.

7. New Morning
   Leominster MA 01453, USA
   Wheat-free cereals.

8. San-J International
   Colonial Heights VA 23834, USA
   Wheat-free tamari soy sauce (less salt, no gluten).

9. Soken Trading Co.
   Sausalito CA 94706, USA
   Rice crackers, snacks, soy products.

10. Westbrae Natural Foods
    Berkeley CA 94706, USA
    100% buckwheat noodles, rice crackers, soy products, wheat-free soy sauce, malts, snacks, unsweetened apple-sauce and condiments.

Available in U.S. stores:

1. Allergy Resources Inc.
   745 Powderhorn, Monument CO 80132, USA
   Amaranth, quinoa, spelt, teff, whole grains, nuts, seeds and flours, a wide variety of food products, pans and non-allergic household products.

2. Ener-G Foods Inc.
   P.O. Box 24723, Seattle WA 98124
   Gluten-free flours, baking mixes, egg and milk substitutes, Jolly Joan products.

3. Featherweight, Chicago Dietetic Supply, Inc.
   La Grange IL 60525
   Gluten-free baking powders, gluten-free flours.

4. Maskal Teff
   1318 Willow, Caldwell ID 83605
   Teff whole grain or flour, in brown or ivory.

5. Now Foods
   Villa Park IL 60181
   Amaranth flour and grain, gluten-free flours, guar gum.

6. Nu-World Amaranth, Inc.
   P.O. Box 2202, Naperville IL 60566
   Amaranth flour and seeds, puffed amaranth, garden seeds.

7. Purity Foods, Inc.
   2871 W. Jolly Road, Okemos MI 48864–3547
   Organic whole grain spelt, spelt flour and pastas.

8. Quinoa Corp.
   24248 Crenshaw Blvd., Ste. 220, Torrance CA 90505
   Whole quinoa seeds and flour, quinoa pastas made with corn.

Available retail/wholesale by mail order:

1. Allergy resources
   62 Firwood Rd., Port Washington NY 11050, USA
   They claim if you can't find an allergy product, they will.
   Amaranth flour, gluten-free flours, oat, barley and tapioca
   flour, guar gum, xanthan gum, arrowroot, mixes, carob,
   calcium carbonate, cream of tartar, milk and egg substitutes, grains and beans, vitamins.

2. Canadian Soya Industries Ltd.
   P.O. Box 69277 Stn. K, Vancouver BC V5K 4W5, Canada
   Same products as Canasoy (page 178). Mail order only to
   areas *without* local health food stores.

3. Illinois Amaranth Company
   Dept. C, R.R. #2, Box 396A, Mundelein IL 60060, USA
   Amaranth flour and grain.

4. Walnut Acres
   Penns Creek PA 17862, USA
   Amaranth flour and grains, variety of gluten-free flours,
   whole grains, legumes, nuts and seeds, dried fruits, variety
   of condiments, organic foods.

FOOD FAMILIES

Some allergy treatments include rotation of foods from different food families, alternating foods every other day or including them in the diet once weekly. Use of these convenient charts will make daily and weekly meal plans easier to create. See allergy books or your doctor for more information on rotation diets.

Plant Food Families

FOOD NAME	FAMILY	FOOD NAME	FAMILY
alfalfa	legume	butternut	walnut
almond	plum	cabbage	mustard
allspice	myrtle	cantaloupe	gourd
aloe	lily	caper	single
anise	parsley	caraway	parsley
apple	apple	cardamom	ginger
apricot	plum	carob	legume
arrowroot	single	carrot	parsley
artichoke	composite	cashew	cashew
asparagus	lily	cauliflower	mustard
avocado	laurel	cayenne	potato
bamboo	cereal	celery	parsley
banana	banana	chard	Swiss
barley	cereal	cherry	plum
basil	mint	chestnut	single
bay leaf	laurel	chicory	chicory
beans	legume	chili	potato
beet	beet	chives	lily
blackberry	rose	chocolate	stercula
blueberry	heather	cinnamon	laurel
boysenberry	rose	citron	citrus
brazil nut	single	clove	myrtle
broccoli	mustard	cocoa	stercula
Brussels sprout	mustard	coconut	palm
buckwheat	buckwheat	coffee	single

FOOD NAME	FAMILY	FOOD NAME	FAMILY
cola	stercula	huckleberry	heather
collard	mustard	Jerusalem	
corn	cereal	artichoke	composite
coriander	parsley	kale	mustard
cottonseed	mallow	kohlrabi	mustard
cowpea	legume	kumquat	citrus
cranberry	heather	lambs quarters	beet
cream of tartar	grape	lecithin	legume
cucumber	gourd	leek	lily
cumin	parsley	lemon	citrus
currant	gooseberry	lentil	legume
dandelion	composite	lettuce	composite
date	palm	licorice	legume
dewberry	rose	lime	citrus
dill	parsley	lichi nut	single
eggplant	potato	loganberry	rose
elderberry	single	macadamia	
endive	composite	nut	single
escarole	composite	mace	nutmeg
fennel	parsley	malt	cereal
fig	mulberry	mango	cashew
filbert	single	maple	single
garlic	single	marjoram	mint
ginger	ginger	melons	gourd
ginseng	single	millet	cereal
gooseberry	gooseberry	mint	mint
grape	grape	molasses	cereal
grapefruit	citrus	mulberry	mulberry
green pepper	potato	mushroom	fungus
guava	myrtle	muskmelon	gourd
hazelnut	single	mustard	mustard
hickory	walnut	mustard greens	mustard
honey	single	nectarine	plum
hop	mulberry	New Zealand	
horehound	mint	(velvet-leafed)	
horseradish	mustard	spinach	purslane

FOOD NAME	FAMILY	FOOD NAME	FAMILY
nutmeg	nutmeg	raspberry	rose
oat	cereal	red pepper	potato
okra	mallow	rhubarb	buckwheat
olive	single	rice	cereal
onion	lily	rutabaga	mustard
orange	citrus	rye	cereal
oregano	mint	safflower	composite
papaya	single	saffron	single
paprika	potato	sage	mint
parsley	parsley	sago	palm
parsnip	parsley	salsify	composite
pea	legume	sassafras	laurel
peach	plum	savoury	mint
peanut	legume	sesame	single
pear	apple	sorghum	cereal
pecan	walnut	sorrel	buckwheat
pepper, black	single	soybean	legume
pepper, white	single	spearmint	mint
pepper, green	potato	spinach	beet
pepper, red	potato	squash	gourd
peppermint	mint	strawberry	rose
persimmon	single	sugar cane	cereal
pimento	myrtle	sunchoke	composite
pineapple	single	sunflower	composite
pine nut	single	sweet potato	single
pistachio	cashew	tangerine	citrus
plantain	banana	tapioca	single
plum	plum	taro	single
pomegranate	single	tea	single
potato	potato	thyme	mint
prune	plum	tobaccco	potato
pumpkin	gourd	tomato	potato
purslane	purslane	tragacanth gum	legume
quince	apple	triticale	cereal
radish	mustard	turmeric	ginger
raisin (grape)	grape	turnip	mustard

FOOD NAME	FAMILY	FOOD NAME	FAMILY
vanilla	single	wheat	cereal
walnut	walnut	wild rice	cereal
water chestnut	single	wintergreen	heather
watercress	mustard	yam	single
watermelon	gourd	yeast	fungus

Plant Foods According to Food Family

Apple	apple	**Chicory**	chicory
	pear	**Citrus**	citron
	quince		grapefruit
Banana	banana		kumquat
	plantain		lemon
Beet	beet		lime
	chard		orange
	lambs quarters		tangerine
	spinach	**Composite**	artichoke
Buckwheat	buckwheat		chicory
	rhubarb		dandelion
	sorrel		endive
Cashew	cashew		escarole
	mango		Jerusalem
	pistachio		artichoke
Cereal	bamboo		(sunchoke)
	barley		lettuce
	corn		salsify
	millet		sunflower
	oats	**Fungus**	mushroom
	rice		yeast
	rye	**Ginger**	cardamom
	sorghum		ginger
	sugar cane		turmeric
Cereal (cont.)	triticale	**Gooseberry**	currant
	wheat		gooseberry
	wild rice	**Gourd**	cantaloupe

Gourd (cont.)	cucumber		peppermint
	melons		sage
	pumpkin		savoury
	squash		spearmint
Grape	cream of tartar		thyme
	grape	**Mulberry**	fig
	raisin		hop
Heather	blueberry		mulberry
	cranberry	**Mustard**	broccoli
	huckleberry		Brussels sprout
	wintergreen		cabbage
Laurel	avocado		cauliflower
	bay leaf		collard
	cinnamon		horseradish
	sassafras		kale
Legumes	beans		kohlrabi
	carob		mustard
	cowpea		mustard green
	lentil		radish
	licorice		rutabaga
	peas		turnip
	peanuts		watercress
	soybean	**Myrtle**	allspice
	tragacanth gum		clove
Lily	aloe		guava
	asparagus		pimento
	chives	**Nutmeg**	nutmeg
	garlic		mace
	leek	**Palm**	coconut
	onion		date
Mallow	cottonseed		sago
	okra	**Parsley**	anise
Mint	basil		caraway
	horehound		carrot
	marjoram		celery
	mint		coriander
	oregano		cumin

Parsley
(cont.)

dill
fennel
parsley
parsnip

Plum

almond
apricot
cherry
nectarine
peach
plum (prune)

Potato

cayenne
chili
eggplant
green pepper
paprika
potato
red pepper
tobacco
tomato

Purslane

New Zealand
(velvet-leafed)
spinach
purslane

Rose

blackberry
boysenberry
dewberry
loganberry
raspberry
strawberry

Stercula

chocolate
cocoa
cola

Walnut

butternut
hickory nut
pecan
walnut

Single Food Families

arrowroot
brazil nut
caper
chestnut
coffee
elderberry
filbert (hazelnut)
ginseng
honey
lichi nut
macademia nut
maple
olive
papaya
pepper (black)
pepper (white)
persimmon
pine nut
pineapple
pomegranate
saffron
sesame
sweet potato
tapioca
taro
tea
vanilla
water chestnut

ALLERGY BOOK LIST

Recipe Books

The Self-Help Cookbook, Marjorie Hurt Jones, R.N. Pennsylvania: Rodale Press, 1984. ISBN 0-87857-505-7.

Dr. Mandell's Allergy-Free Cookbook, Fran Gare Mandell. New York: Simon & Schuster (Pocket Books), 1981. ISBN 0-671-83603-X.

Allergy Cooking, Marion L. Conrad. New York: Jove Publications, 1978. ISBN 0-515-05738-X.

Food Intolerance, Robert Buist. Great Britain: Prism Press, 1984. ISBN 0-907061-68-0.

Creative Cooking Without Wheat, Milk and Eggs, Ruth R. Shattuck. New Jersey: A. S. Barnes and Co., 1980. ISBN 0-498-02047-9.

Freedom from Allergy, Dr. Ron Greenberg, M.D. and Angela Nori. Vancouver: Gordon Soules Book Publishers, 1990. ISBN 0-88925-905-4.

Coping with Food Allergy, Claude A. Frazier, M.D. New York: New York Times Books Co. (Quadrangle Books), 1980. ISBN 0-8129-6278-8.

The Milk-Free and Milk/Egg-Free Cookbook, Isobel S. Sainsbury, M.D. New York: Arco Publishing, 1980. ISBN 0-668-04701-1.

Good Food, Milk Free, Grain Free, Cherry Hills. Connecticut: Keats Publishing, 1980. ISBN 0-87983-201-0.

Good Food, Gluten Free, Cherry Hills. Connecticut: Keats Publishing, 1976. ISBN 0-87983-103-0.

Gluten-Free Cooking, Rita Greer. England: Thorsons Publishers, 1978. ISBN 0-7225-0435-7.

Information Books

The Complete Guide to Food Allergy and Intolerance, Dr. Jonathan Brostoff and Linda Gamlin. England: Bloomsbury Publishing, 1989. ISBN 0-7475-0566-7.

How to Control Your Allergies, Robert Forman, Ph.D. New York: Larchmont Books, 1983. ISBN 0-915962-29-2.

Dr. Mandell's Allergy Relief System by Dr. Marshall Mandell and Lynne Waller Scanlon. New York: Simon & Schuster (Pocket Books), 1980. ISBN 0-671-43028-9.

The Allergy Self-Help Book, Sharon Faeltenand and the editors of *Prevention* magazine. Pennsylvania: Rodale Press, 1983. ISBN 0-87857-458-1.

An Alternative Approach to Allergies, Theron G. Randolph, M.D. and Ralph W. Moss, Ph.D. New York: Bantam Books, 1982. ISBN 0-553-20830-6.

The Allergy Handbook, Dr. Keith Mumby. England: Thorsons Publishers, 1988. ISBN 0-7225-1657-6.

Food Allergies Made Simple, Phyllis Austin, Agatha Thrash, M.D. and Calvin Thrash, M.D. Michigan: Family Health Publications, 1985. ISBN 0-942658-08-6.

Hidden Food Allergies, Stephen Astor, M.D. New York: Avery Publishing Group, 1988. ISBN 0-89529-369-2.

The Type 1/Type 2 Allergy Relief Program, Alan Scott Levin, M.D. and Merla Zellerbach. California: Tarcher, 1983. ISBN 0-87477-328-8.

The Allergy Encyclopedia, ed. Asthma and Allergy Foundation of America and Craig T. Norback. New York: New American Library (Plume), 1981. ISBN 0-452-25270-9.

(How You Too Can) Outsmart Your Food Allergies, Beverly D. Chiu. B.C.: Yellow Hat Press, 1987. ISBN 0-921937-01-6.

Goodbye Allergies, Judge Tom R. Blaine. New Jersey: Citadel Press, 1976. ISBN 0-8065-0639-3.

A Consumer's Dictionary of Food Additives, Ruth Winter. New York: Crown, 1978. ISBN 0-517-531615.

The Food Intolerance Diet Book, Elizabeth Workman, Dr. Virginia Alun-Jones and Dr. John Hunter. Martin Dunitz Ltd., 1989. ISBN 0948269-16-2.

The Allergy Cookbook: Diets Unlimited for Limited Diets, Allergy Information Association Canada. U.K.: Methuen, 1983. ISBN 0-458-80690-0.

Children's Allergies

Healthier Children, Barbara Kahan. New Canaan CT: Keats Publishing Inc., 1990. ISBN 0-87983-475-7.
Tracking Down Hidden Food Allergies, William G. Crook, M.D. Tennessee: Professional Books, 1980. ISBN 0-933478-05-4.
Parents' Guide to Allergy in Children, Claude A. Frazier, M.D. New York: Grosset & Dunlap, 1978. ISBN 0-448-16180 X.

Tofu Recipe Books

The Book of Tofu, William Shurtleff and Akiko Aoyagi. New York: Ballantine, 1980. ISBN 0-345-27809-7.
Tofu Quick & Easy, Louise Hagler. Tennessee: The Book Publishing Co., 1986. ISBN 0-913990-50-1.
Tofu Madness, Nancy Olszewski. Washington: Island Spring Publishing, Inc., 1982. ISBN
Tofu Goes West, Gary Landgrebe. California: Fresh Press, 1982. ISBN 0-9601398-2-6.
Tofu Cookery, Louise Hagler. Tennessee: The Book Publishing Co., 1982. ISBN 0-913990-38-8.
Tofu — Everybody's Guide, Stephen Cherniske. East Woodstock CT: Mother's Inn Centre for Creative Living, 1980.

Specialty Cookbooks

Wild Rice for All Seasons Cookbook, Beth Anderson. Manitoba: Tundra Wild Rice Inc., 1988. ISBN 0-961-00300-6.
Quinoa the Supergrain, Rebecca Wood. New York: Japan Publications USA, 1989. ISBN 0-87040-780-5.
The New American Vegetable Cookbook, Georgeanne Brennan, Isaac Cronin and Charlotte Glenn. New York: Aris Books, 1988. ISBN 0-943186-25-0.
America's Best Vegetable Recipes, food editors of *Farm Journal*. New York: Doubleday, 1970. ISBN 0-385-03155-6.

Country Kitchen Collection, Silver Hills Guest House. R.R. 2, Mable Lake Rd., Lumby, B.C. ISBN 0–88925–933–X.

Sugar Substitute Cookbooks

Sweet and Sugar Free, Karen E. Barkie. New York: St. Martin's Press, 1982. ISBN 0–312–78066–4.
The Sugarless Cookbook, Nellie G. Hum. Regina: Centax Canada, 1987. ISBN 0–919845–52–5.
Fresh Fruit Drinks, Lorraine Whiteside. New York: Thorsons Publishers, 1984. ISBN 0–7225–0836–0.

Allergy Recipe Booklets

Super Foods, Marjorie Hurt Jones, R.N. Idaho: Mast Enterprises, 1990. No ISBN.
All-Natural Allergy Snack-Book, Linda Reimann. Colorado: Royal Publications, Inc., 1981. ISBN 0–918738–06–7.
Baking with Amaranth, Marge Jones, R.N. Deerfield, Illinois, 1983. No ISBN.
Amaranth Recipes, Patti Bosomworth and Beverly Newton. B.C.: Sisu Enterprises Ltd., n.d. No ISBN.
Natural Sweetener Recipe Book (fruit juice sweetener recipes), Mystic Lake Dairy. Redmond, Washington, n.d. No ISBN.
Alfa-Milk, Charles A. Zumwait. Orono ID: ALFA Better Health Foods, 1982. No ISBN.

Allergy Information Booklets

Allergies Revisited, Dr. Donsbach. California: International Institute of Natural Health Sciences, 1980. No ISBN.
Are You Drinking Homogenized Milk?, Kurt A. Oster, M.D. Glen Head NY: Sunflower Publishing Co., 1981. No ISBN.
Your Child and Allergy, William G. Crook, M.D. Tennessee: Professional Books, 1977. No ISBN.

INDEX